THE OFFICIAL

LICENSE

PLATE BOOK 2000

A COMPLETE PLATE IDENTIFICATION RESOURCE

License Plates
U.S.A., Canada & Mexico

A REGISTRY OF 1,000
COLOR ILLUSTRATIONS

by Thomson C. Murray

designed by William L Cummings
graphic design by
Jonathan Golstein
Michael Masotti

ISBN 1-886777-03-9

INTERSTATE DIRECTORY PUBLISHING CO. INC.
420 Jericho Turnpike-Suite 300
Jericho NY 11753
1-800-347-0473 or 516-822-5966 Fax 5962
www.idpubco.com

The author wishes to thank Larry Greenberg and The American Association of Motor Vehicle Administrators for their help both with this and previous editions. The Motor Vehicle Departments of all 51 U.S and 13 Canadian jurisdictions have been wonderful this year as in the past. A word of appreciation to the Turtle Mountain Tribal Council for granting permission to include their plate. A special word of thanks is due to all my friends at 3M Corporation, the firm who developed the reflective sheeting that makes all these beautiful graphic plates possible.

A special appreciation to: my fellow members of ALPCA including: Alfonso Baca, Michael Wiener, Roy Carson, John Northup, David R. Wilson, Chuck Sakryd, Andrew Apgar, Keith Marvin,Don Merrill, Mike McEnaney, Mike Natale, Donald Stow, Arlene Jang, Bob Bittner, Jim Fox, Dave Fraser, Darrell Dady, Kit Sage, Rich Bell and Richard Dragon.Other key contributors are Mike Masotti, Bill Cummings, Jon Goldstein, Peggy Mallon ,Scott Lambert, Jeff Gould ,Clay Acup and Barbara Cooney ... all part of the very special team that makes this book and ID Pubco possible.

Dedicated to
Mary Thompson Murray
lovingly remembered as

Geggie

The license plates illustrated in this book are a representative sample selected by the author. They illustrate a typical type of plate issued by a jurisdiction. If the alpha and/or numeric characters duplicate a particular plate currently in use it is strictly coincidental. The material in this book was compiled from information provided by Motor Vehicle authorities. Interstate Directory Publishing Company Inc. is not responsible for any inadvertent inaccuracies or omissions.

ISBN 1-886777-02- 0

Introduction

License plates often have hidden meanings that can be recognized by law enforcement, serious collectors and motor vehicle authorities. This book explains how states and provinces code their plates so you, like the authorities, will be able to look at a plate and tell such things as:

In what county a vehicle is registered
Occupation of the owner
Special plates and what they mean
Age, weight and vehicle use restrictions
How to recognize a rental vehicle
State, City, Federal Government, Diplomatic codes
Indian tribes
First initial of the owners last name or birth month

Also:
Addresses and phone numbers for all motor vehicle departments

How to "read" a license plate

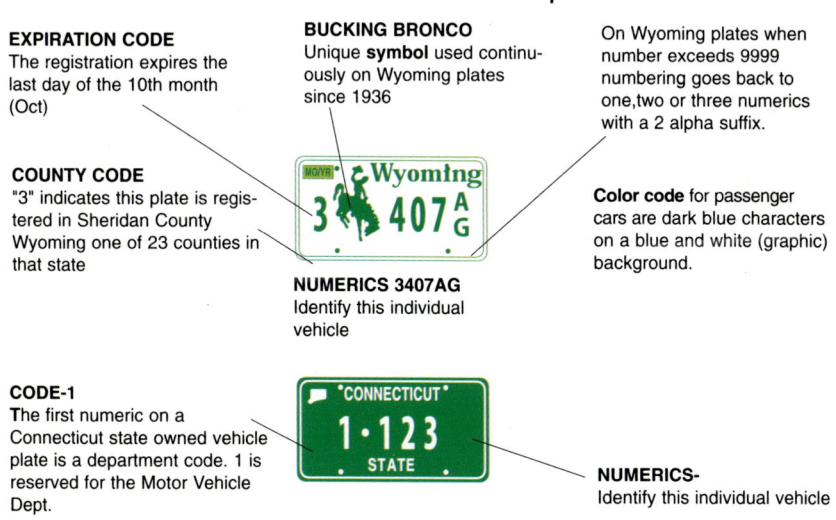

EXPIRATION CODE
The registration expires the last day of the 10th month (Oct)

BUCKING BRONCO
Unique **symbol** used continuously on Wyoming plates since 1936

On Wyoming plates when number exceeds 9999 numbering goes back to one, two or three numerics with a 2 alpha suffix.

COUNTY CODE
"3" indicates this plate is registered in Sheridan County Wyoming one of 23 counties in that state

Color code for passenger cars are dark blue characters on a blue and white (graphic) background.

NUMERICS 3407AG
Identify this individual vehicle

CODE-1
The first numeric on a Connecticut state owned vehicle plate is a department code. 1 is reserved for the Motor Vehicle Dept.

NUMERICS-
Identify this individual vehicle

1. Look at the color combinations. Each section explains how jurisdictions use color combinations to distinguish classes of vehicle.
2. If you see a caption (a word embossed or screen-printed on a plate) you do not understand, look under the **Distinctive Caption section and it will be explained. For example JITNEY in Rhode Island is a caption for a repossessor plate.**
3. **Codes- Look at the combination of alpha and numeric characters (letters and numbers) and check the code section to see if there are any hidden meanings.**

LICENSE PLATES AND HOW TO *READ* THEM

The popular name for the metal plate affixed to a vehicle is a "license plate." In many states, particularly in the South, these are commonly referred to as "license tags." Actually the vehicle is not licensed, the driver is. Every vehicle is "registered" with authorities, and the metal plate is issued to identify each particular vehicle and indicate that it has met certain conditions and the owner has paid required registration fees and taxes. The driver is "licensed" and the metal plate is a "registration plate," but for over ninety years the public has used the term "license plate" and we won't try to correct this now.

License plates are issued to indicate proper registration of a vehicle. They also often contain codes which can tell you a lot about the vehicle and the owner. In fact there is an incredible "hidden language" of license plates which this book has been designed to explain.

Although every state and provincial motor vehicle administration uses a different system to issue plates and assign numbers, they all recognize the need for law enforcement authorities to distinguish classes of vehicles by simply glancing at the plate. There are three methods to make these distinctions:

COLOR- Different combinations are used for classes of vehicles.

CAPTIONS- Words are embossed or screen-printed to give special information

CODES- Series of letters and numbers (alpha, numeric characters) used in the plate numbering system that are reserved for special identification

The material in this book has been gathered from Motor Vehicle administrations of all 50 states, District of Columbia, 12 Canadian provinces and territories as well as contributions from members of Automobile License Plate Collectors Association (ALPCA). It is organized to explain how every jurisdiction (state or province) uses these three methods to help authorities "read" a license plate and instantly tell if it is a valid registration, what county it comes from, its weight class, and/or use restrictions, the driver's occupation, and any other special information that may be available about the owner and his vehicle.

PASSENGER CARS

All U.S. and Canadian jurisdictions currently issue permanent or semi-permanent license plates that are used for a number of years and revalidated with decals or windshield decals. Of the 51 U.S. jurisdictions, 32 issue two plates, while the remaining 19 require only one plate per vehicle. The things to look for on license plates are:

COUNTY CODES
OCCUPATION CODES
EXPIRATION CODES
GOVERNMENT DEPARTMENT CODES
CODES RESERVED FOR SPECIAL GROUPS AND OFFICIALS

In many states you can tell in which county a vehicle is registered, if the owner is a member of a special group or organization, and the age and weight of the vehicle. All this information and much more is available from just looking at a license plate and referring to this book.

TRUCKS TRAILERS AND OTHER HEAVY VEHICLES

Trucks, truck tractors, buses, trailers and other heavy vehicles, unlike private passenger cars, must pay a variety of taxes based on weight, miles driven and fuel consumption in addition to registration fees.This is why commercial license plates are often a different color and sometimes changed more frequently than passenger plates.

Every state has at least two sources of revenue that is collected from commercial vehicles: registration fees and fuel consumption taxes. Some states have a third level of taxation based on a formula of miles run and tons carried.

In addition to a registration license plate, a commercial vehicle operating only within the state where it is registered must display a decal or plate showing registration for the payment of fuel and any other taxes required by the particular state. This is usually done by a small plate issued by the Public Service Commission (PSC) or Tax Commissioner, or by a decal on the cab or bumper of the vehicle.

VEHICLES OPERATING INTERSTATE

Private passenger cars can cross state lines and drive freely anywhere within the United States because every state has agreed to honor the registration of a passenger vehicle registered in every other state. This is called full reciprocity.

Commercial vehicles do not enjoy this same freedom of movement over state lines.

States rely heavily on commercial vehicle registration and tax revenue to defray the cost of highway construction and maintenance. They insist that all trucks and other heavy vehicles using their highways pay their fair share. As a result, a commercial or heavy vehicle cannot operate in another state unless there is some agreement between the two states providing for reciprocity (sharing of registration fees). This sharing of registration and tax revenue is called apportionment or proration.

Currently most states have some sort of agreement with every other state to grant full reciprocity or share registration fees and tax revenue based on actual highway use. This is a complicated problem and difficult for both state authorities and the trucking industry to administer and enforce. This situation is one reason you often see multiple plates and decals on vehicles operating interstate .

In recent years 48 states and Alberta, British Columbia, and Saskatchewan have joined the International Registration Plan (IRP) where only one license plate captioned APPORTIONED is issued by the state where the vehicle is based. This is the only plate that has to be displayed by heavy vehicles operating interstate within the member states.

PLATES AND PARKING FOR THE DISABLED

The automobile gives a disabled person in the United States the chance to enjoy independence and mobility. They are given special parking privileges, and every effort is made to meet their needs and still not inconvenience the general public.

The familiar wheelchair symbol is used worldwide. The official name of this symbol is International Symbol of Access (ISA) and appears on signs, placards and license plates to identify vehicles transporting disabled persons and the parking areas reserved for their use.

Until 1991 there were no uniform guidelines covering the administration of special parking for the disabled. Every state handled the situation in their individual manner. Some of the problems are abuse of special parking by unauthorized people using disabled plates and special parking plates designed and issued in one state were often not recognized or honored in other states. The Department of Transportation (DOT) developed a uniform system for disabled parking which became federal law March 11, 1991. Under this law every qualified applicant for special parking privileges will have the choice of either a special plate embossed with the ISA or a parking placard to hang from the rearview mirror on the inside of the vehicle. The advantage of the placard is it can be moved to any vehicle, and the car remains unmarked when the placard is not displayed. The law also permits two placards to be issued to one individual if needed.

Blue placards are issued only for permanent disability and are renewed periodically by the issuing jurisdiction.

Red placards are issued for temporary disabilities and are valid for a maximum period of six months.

These representative samples of disabled persons parking permits from two jurisdictions (Washington and Montana) were provided through the courtesy of:

The American Association of Motor Vehicle Administrators, Arlington VA

Actual size of placard is 3 1/2 x 9 1/4 in.

Manufacturing and Reflectorization

It is still true that most license plates are manufactured in correctional institutions, however there are some private contractors who also make plates for some states (Alaska, Arkansas Delaware, Hawaii,Illinois, Kansas, Mississippi and Oregon).

License plates are made by stamping letters and numbers into a metal blank and then roller-coating the raised portion with a contrasting color ink. In the 1940's two New England states added a reflective coating to their plates to make them easier to see at night. The reflective coating is made of millions of tiny glass beads that refract (bend) the light which reflects back many times brighter than from a plain painted surface.

Plates that are painted and have the reflective glass beads added to just the raised characters are partially-reflective. New materials have been developed that can be printed many colors and stamped and still retain the reflective quality of the glass beads. This special sheeting is pre-printed and then adhered to the metal blank and stamped. The raised characters are colored with ink and the whole plate is coated with a clear protective material. This type of plate is referred to as fully-reflectorized.

Reflectorization is an important safety factor and of significant value to law enforcement. Just consider a police officer checking isolated parking lots at night . With reflectorized plates identification can quickly and easily be achieved with headlights or a spotlight from a patrol car . Fully reflectorized plates can be seen at long distance at night, and can be very colorful. The only drawback is special reflective sheeting adds to the expense of manufacturing plates.

DIPLOMATIC LICENSE PLATES

 In 1985 the United States Department of State began issuing red white and blue plates to vehicles owned by foreign missions. Prefix **C,D,S** is used nationwide, suffix **A,C,D,S** is reserved for The United Nations.The 2 letters used in the numbering system is a country code.

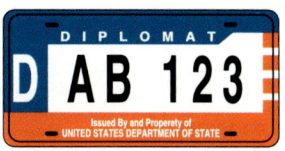

AA CONGO	**FP** MOROCCO	**KX** SUDAN	**QZ** INDONESIA
AC IVORY COAST	**FR** PHILIPPINES	**LC** VENEZUELA	**RB** RWANDA
AF JAPAN	**FS** NETHERLANDS	**LG** TURKEY	**RC** ST VINCENT
AH MADAGASCAR	**FT** QATAR	**LD** VIET NAM	**RD** SENEGAL
AJ PANAMA	**FV** SRI LANKA	**LH** ISRAEL	**RL** URUGUAY
AK CAPE VERDE	**FW** VATICAN	**LJ** ISRAEL	**SG** ISRAEL
AQ SYRIA	**FX** SIERRA LEONE	**LK** DEL. TO EEC	**ST** DOMINICA
AU UGANDA	**FY** SOUTH AFRICA	**LW** GERMANY	**SX** USSR
AV ISRAEL	**FZ** SURINAME	**MK** DJIBOUTI	**TC** MALI
AW ORG. OF AFRICAN UNITY	**GC** SWEDEN	**ML** DIEGO GARCIA	**TF** ALGERIA
	GD UKRAINE	**MN** COMOROS	**TG** CANADA
BL SOUTH AFRICA	**GG** ZAMBIA	**MP** BAHAMAS	**TH** EGYPT
BY SOLOMON ISLANDS	**GM** TURKEY	**MQ** MONACO	**TJ** GERMANY
	GP ALBANIA	**MW** MALDIVES	**TK** NETH. ANTIL.
BZ IRAQ	**GQ** NORTH KOREA	**NA** OMAN	**TL** EL SALVADOR
CB CAMBODIA	**HL** ST. LUCIA	**NB** NEW GUINEA	**TM** ICELAND
CC ETHIOPIA	**HN** MONGOLIA	**NC** PARAGUAY	**TN** NEPAL
CS AFGHANISTAN	**HV** BELGIUM	**ND** ROMANIA	**TP** MAURITANIA
CT BHUTAN	**HW** GUATEMALA	**NQ** ANGOLA	**TR** ITALY
CU BOTSWANA	**HX** BENIN	**PA** AUSTRIA	**TS** IRAQ
CV BURMA	**HY** GUINEA BISSAU	**PB** BARBADOS	**TT** GUYANA
CW CAMEROON	**HZ** HAITI	**PC** BELIZE	**TU** GUINEA
CX BURUNDI	**JB** HONDURAS	**PD** BERMUDA	**TV** GHANA
CY CHINA	**JC** KUWAIT	**PF** BOLIVIA	**TW** GAMBIA
DA COLOMBIA	**JD** MAURITIUS	**PG** BYELORUSSIA	**TX** FINLAND
DB COSTA RICA	**JF** NIGERIA	**PH** CZECH.	**TY** GRENADA
DC CUBA	**JG** PORTUGAL	**PI** ISRAEL	**TZ** PERU
DD CYPRUS	**JH** SOMALIA	**PK** NORWAY	**UA** BAHRAIN
DF DOM. REP	**JJ** CHAD	**PL** CHILE	**UF** ESTONIA
DG ECUADOR	**JK** TURKEY	**PM** BRUNEI	**UH** SPAIN
DH FR. CARIBBEAN	**JM** YUGOSLAVIA	**PR** ARGENTINA	**UX** TRINIDAD & TOBAGO
DI ISRAEL.	**JP** TUNISIA	**PS** ZIMBABWE	
DJ FRANCE	**JQ** TOGO	**PV** ZAIRE	**VF** THAILAND
DK GREECE	**KG** EQU.GUINEA	**QA** N. YEMEN	**VG** TANZANIA
DL INDIA	**KH** HUNGARY	**QD** BURKINA FASO	**VH** SWITZERLAND
DM IRAN	**KJ** LITHUANIA	**QL** ST. KITTS	**VJ** BRAZIL
DN DENMARK	**KK** FIJI	**QM** BULGARIA	**VK** SINGAPORE
DP BANGLADESH	**KL** JORDAN	**QN** LAOS	**VL** SWAZILAND
FC FORMER USSR	**KM** JAMAICIA	**QP** LATVIA	**WB** U.A.E.
FF ANTIGUA	**KN** GABON	**QQ** LESOTHO	**WD** S KOREA
FG CEN.AF.REP.	**KP** LUXEMBOURG	**QR** MALAWI	**WM** W. SAMOA
FH IRELAND	**KR** MALAYSIA	**QS** MOZAMBIQUE	**WZ** UNIT. KNGDM
FI ISRAEL	**KS** MEXICO	**QT** NEW ZEALAND	**XF** TURKEY
FJ LEBANON	**KT** NAMIBIA	**QU** NICARAGUA	**XZ** AUSTRALIA
FK KENYA	**KU** SAO TOME / PRINCIPE	**QV** NIGER	**YM** HONG KONG
FL LIBERIA		**QW** POLAND	
FM LIBYA	**KV** SAUDI ARABIA	**QX** PAKISTAN	
FN MALTA	**KW** SEYCHELLES	**QY** S. YEMEN	

UNITED STATES GOVERNMENT VEHICLES

The General Services Administration (GSA) maintains vehicles in motor pools across the country for official use of Government agencies and departments. All plates are blue on white. The prefix indicates vehicle type.

G11 - Sedans; intermediate; subcompact
G12 - Sedans; compact
G14 - Sedans; standard
G21 - Station wagons; subcompact/ compact
G23 - Station wagons; standard
G31 - Ambulances; buses
G41 - Trucks- cargo 1/2 ton and under (4x2)
G42 - Trucks- cargo 3/4 ton (4x2)
G43 - Trucks- cargo 1 ton (4x2)

G61 - Trucks - cargo 1/2 ton and under (4x4)
G62 - Trucks - cargo 3/4 ton (4x4)
G63 - Trucks - cargo 1 ton (4x4)
G71 - Trucks - cargo 12,500 - 23,999 GVW
G81 - Trucks - cargo 24,000+ GVW gasoline
G82 - Trucks - Cargo 24,000+ GVW diesel
G91 - Trucks, trailers , semi-trailers (special purpose type vehicles)

Federal Government owned vehicles owned by individual departments can be identified by the alpha prefix code as follows:

A - Agriculture
ACT - Action
AF - Air Force
C - Commerce
CA - Civil Aeronautics Board
CE - Corps of Engineers
CPSC - Consumer Product Safety Comm.
CS - Civil Service Commission
D - Defense
DA - Defense Contract Audit Agency
DOT - Dept. of Transportation
DA - Defense Supply Agency
E - Energy Research & Development Admin.
EO - Executive Office of the President
   Council of Economic Advisors
   National Security Council
   Office of Management & Budget
EPA - Environmental Protection Agency
EPS - Executive Protection Services
FA - Federal Aviation Administration
FC - Federal Communications Comm.
FD - Federal Deposit Insurance Corp.
FM - Federal Mediation &Conciliation Serv.
FP - Federal Power Commission
FR - Federal Reserve System
FT - Federal Trade Commission
G - Interagency Motor Pool System
GA - General Accounting Office
GP - Government Printing Office
GS - General Services Administration
H - Housing & Urban Development
HW - Health, Education & Welfare

I - Interior
IA - Information Agency
IBC- International Boundary Commission
IC - Interstate Commerce Commission
J - Justice
JB - Judicial Branch
L - Labor
LA - D of C Redevelopment Land Agency
LB - Legislative Branch
N - Navy
NA - Nat'l. Aeronautics & Space Admin.
NG - National Guard Bureau
NH - Nat'l Cap. Housing Authority
NL - National Labor Relations Board
NP - Nat'l Cap. Planning Comm.
NRC - Nuclear Regulatory Comm.
NS - National Science Commission
OEO - Office Economic Opportunity
P - Postal Service
PC -Panama Canal Company
RB - Renegotiation Board
RR - Railroad Retirement Board
S - State Department
SB - Small Business Administration
SE - Securities & Exchange Commission
SH - Soldiers & Sailor"s Home
SI - Smithsonian Institution Ntl Gallery Art.
T - Treasury
TV - Tennessee Valley Authority
VA - Veterans Administration,
W - Army

SAMPLE LICENSE PLATES

A good way to begin a license plate collection is to order a sample plate from each state and province.This book lists the address of every Motor Vehicle Department. If you write them, they will often send you a sample plate for a modest fee. These fees may change.

ALABAMA- $ 3.00
ALASKA- $ 3.00
ARIZONA-$ *6.50
ARKANSAS-** FREE
CALIFORNIA- $12.00
COLORADO- $ 3.00
CONNECTICUT- $ 5.00
DELAWARE- $ 7.00
FLORIDA- FREE
GEORGIA-NO samples
HAWAII-$ 10.00
IDAHO- $ 12.00
ILLINOIS-$ 3.00
INDIANA-$ *4.00
IOWA- $ 3.00
KANSAS- $ 5.50
KENTUCKY- $ 5.00
LOUISIANA-$ 9.50
MAINE-$ 5.00
MARYLAND - FREE
MASSACHUSETTS - $10.00
MICHIGAN- $ 5.00
MINNESOTA- $ 3.00
MISSISSIPPI-$2.00
MISSOURI-$ 7.50
MONTANA- $ 7.50
NEBRASKA- $ 5.00
NEVADA- $ 2.00
NEW HAMPSHIRE- $ 5.00
NEW JERSEY- $ 5.00
NEW MEXICO- $ 5.00
NEW YORK- $5.00
NORTH CAROLINA- $ 10.00
NORTH DAKOTA- $ 5.00
OHIO - FREE
OKLAHOMA- $ 2.00
OREGON- $ 2.50
PENNSYLVANIA- $ 5.00
RHODE ISLAND - $ 2.00
SOUTH CAROLINA - $ 10.00
SOUTH DAKOTA - *$ 3.00
TENNESSEE- FREE
TEXAS- $ 6.90
UTAH - $ 5.00
VERMONT - $ 10.00
VIRGINIA - $ 10.00
WASHINGTON-** FREE
WEST VIRGINIA- $ 5.00
WISCONSIN - $ 2.00
WYOMING - $ 2.50
*Includes postage cost
**expired plate available

CANADA
ALBERTA- $ 10.42 CDN
BRITISH COLUMBIA- $ 10.70 CDN
MANITOBA-FREE
NEW BRUNSWICK- FREE
NEWF.& LAB.- $ 10.00
NORTHWEST TERR.- $ 10.00
NOVA SCOTIA- $ 5.35
ONTARIO- $15.00 CDN
PRINCE ED. ISL.-$ 16.00
QUEBEC- $ 5.00
SASKATCHEWAN- $ 10.00 CDN
YUKON- $ 5.35 CDN

When writing for sample plates it is important to note that policies governing sample plate issuance and pricing can and do change often, It is advisable to send a money order - many jurisdictions do not accept personal checks. Many states offer a variety of passenger and non-passenger sample and/or expired plates as well as expired and sample validation decals.

GUAM
DEPT. OF REVENUE & TAXATION
VEHICLE REGISTRATION BRANCH
855 W MARINE DRIVE
AGANA GU 96910
SAMPLE PLATE $5.00

US VIRGIN ISLANDS
POLICE DEPT, CRIMINAL JUSTICE COMPLEX,
VETERANS DRIVE
CHARLOTTE AMALIE , ST THOMAS VI 00802, ATTN MOTOR VEHICLE BUREAU
SAMPLE PLATE $23.00

DISTRICT OF COLUMBIA-
SAMPLE PLATES ARE NO LONGER AVAILABLE.

ALABAMA

POLICE PATCH

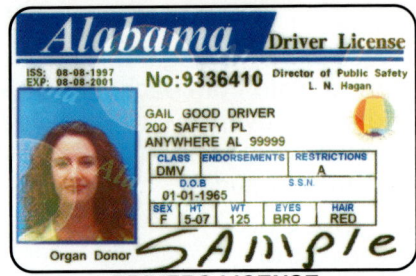

DRIVERS LICENSE

PASSENGER PLATES

PASSENGER
BASE

PERSONALIZED

HANDICAPPED

DISABLED VET

ENVIRONMENT

COLLEGE
AUBURN
UNIVERSITY

COLLEGE
CRIMSON TIDE

AID TO
EDUCATION

CHILDREN'S
TRUST

NATIONAL
GUARD

WILDLIFE

AGRICULTURE

TRUCK AND TRAILER PLATES

APPORTIONED
TRUCK
2000 EXPIRE

APPORTIONED
TRUCK
2001 EXPIRE

TRUCK ANNUAL
PLATE

TRAILER
ANNUAL PLATE

PLATE VALIDATION

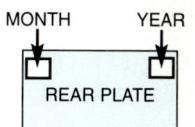

MONTH YEAR

REAR PLATE

www.ador.state.al.us/ motorvehicle/MVD

"The Heart of Dixie" issues one fully-reflectorized license plate for all vehicles. A county code system is in use, and new graphic design passenger car plates were issued in 1997.

Distinctive captions:

ANTIQUE VEHICLE - Collector's vehicle 30 years or older
HELPING SCHOOLS - School fund raising plate
TRANSIT- Dealer's transit plate

Codes:

Alabama plates have a numeric county prefix. The counties and (county seats) are:

1. Jefferson (Birmingham)
2. Mobile (Mobile)
3. Montgomery (Montgomery)
4. Autauga (Prattville)
5. Baldwin (Bay Minette)
6. Barbour (Clayton)
7. Bibb (Centreville)
8. Blount (Oneonta)
9. Bullock (Union Springs)
10. Butler (Greenville)
11. Calhoun (Anniston)
12. Chambers (Lafayette)
13. Cherokee (Centre)
14. Chilton (Clanton)
15. Choctaw (Butler)
16. Clarke (Grove Hill)
17. Clay (Ashland)
18. Cleburne (Heflin)
19. Coffee (Elba)
20. Colbert (Tuscumbia)
21. Conecuh (Evergreen)
22. Coosa (Rockford)
23. Covington (Andalusia)
24. Crenshaw (Luverne)
25. Cullman (Cullman)
26. Dale (Ozark)
27. Dallas (Selma)
28. DeKalb (Fort Payne)
29. Elmore (Wetumpka)
30. Escambia (Brewton)
31. Etowah (Gadsden)
32. Fayette (Fayette)
33. Franklin (Russellville)
34. Geneva (Geneva)
35. Greene (Eutaw)
36. Hale (Greensboro)
37. Henry (Abbeville)
38. Houston (Dothan)
39. Jackson (Scottsboro)
40. Lamar (Vernon)
41. Lauderdale (Florence)
42. Lawrence (Moulton)
43. Lee (Opelika)
44. Limestone (Athens)
45. Lowndes (Hayneville)
46. Macon (Tuskegee)
47. Madison (Huntsville)
48. Marengo (Linden)
49. Marion (Hamilton)
50. Marshall (Guntersville)
51. Monroe (Monroeville)
52. Morgan (Decatur)
53. Perry (Marion)
54. Pickens (Carrollton)
55. Pike (Troy)
56. Randolph (Wedowee)
57. Russell (Phenix City)
58. Shelby (Columbiana)
59. Saint. Clair (Ashville)
60. Sumter (Livingston)
61. Talladega (Talladega)
62. Tallapoosa (Dadeville)
63. Tuscaloosa (Tuscaloosa)
64. Walker (Jasper)
65. Washington (Chatom)
66. Wilcox (Camden)
67. Winston (Double Springs)

Alpha prefixes and suffixes reserved for special use:

BB-60 - Chm. Alabama Battleship Comm.
CO- County owned vehicle
D- Dealer
H- Hearse or ambulance
XL-Truck limited to 15 mile use known as "mule tag"
MOH- Medal of Honor recipient
MU- Municipal owned vehicle
POW- Former prisoner of war

PUD- Public utility
RS- Rescue squad
RT- Rental trailer
S- State owned
TR- Trailer
VAA- Vintage vehicles
Z- Taxi

Trucks have a numeric county code and a 2 character class and weight code:

Alpha class code	Numeric indicates max. gross wgt. in thousands of pounds								
	X1	**X2**	**X3**	**X4**	**X5**	**X6**	**X7**	**X8**	**X9**
F-Farm	30	42							
L-Forest prod.	30	42							
X-Truck	12&18	26	33	42	55	64	73.38	80	over80

ALASKA

POLICE PATCH

DRIVERS LICENSE

PASSENGER PLATES

PASSENGER
BASE

PERSONALIZED

OPTIONAL
GRAPHICS

HANDICAPPED

COLLEGIATE
PRINCE WILLIAM
SOUND

MARINE
VETERAN

NATIONAL
GUARD

PEARL
HARBOR
SURVIVOR

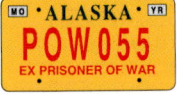

FORMER POW

STATE
LEGISLATOR

WILDLIFE
PROTECTION

TRIBAL PLATE

TRUCK AND TRAILER PLATES

TRUCK

TRAILER

PLATE VALIDATION

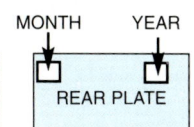  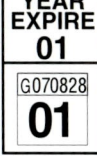

MONTH   YEAR

FRONT PLATE   REAR PLATE

YEAR EXPIRE 00
E070828
00

YEAR EXPIRE 01
G070828
01

www.state.ak.us/dmv

"The Last Frontier" issues two fully-reflectorized license plates. A three alpha - three numeric format is used for all regular issue passenger plates .

Distinctive captions:

THE LAST FRONTIER- State slogan on all but special plates
HISTORICAL- A vehicle at least 30 years old
OFFICIAL USE ONLY - State owned vehicle
OCCASIONAL-Off-road vehicle
PROTECTION - Fish and wildlife protection
PURPLE HEART - Recipient of the Purple Heart Medal
VETERAN - Veteran of Army, Navy, Air Force, Marines, Coast Guard
GOLD RUSH CENTENNIAL - Centennial celebration of Gold Rush Era.

Codes:

Alaska issues 3 alpha - 3 numeric plates to passenger vehicles and 4 numeric- 2 alpha plates to trucks, trailers and buses.

Alpha prefixes and suffixes reserved for special use:

AST - Alaska State Trooper
BAA- CNW - Passenger vehicles
FWP - Fish and Wildlife Protection
HCP - Handicapped person
KL7, WL7 - Ham radio call sign
PWS - Prince William Sound College
UAA, UAF,UAS - Collegiate plates
VAR,VAF,VCG,VNV,VMC - Veteran

BA - DZ - Truck
DL - Dealer
FA - Farm
PA,PC,PD - Trailer (private)
PB, PW - Non-commercial trailer
SA - SF - Commercial trailer

Alaska does not designate county or weight of a vehicle on the license plate.

Alaska Department of Administration, Division of Motor Vehicles
2150 Dowling Road, Anchorage, AK 99507   Tel. 907-269-5559

ARIZONA

POLICE PATCH

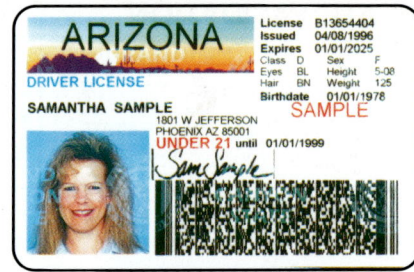

DRIVERS LICENSE

PASSENGER PLATES

PASSENGER BASE

PERSONALIZED

ENVIRONMENT

HANDICAPPED

COLLEGIATE ASU

COLLEGIATE N. ARIZONA

GOVERNMENT

COUNTY PLATE

FORMER POW

CONGRESSIONAL MEDAL OF HONOR

PURPLE HEART

HISTORIC VEHICLE

TRUCK AND TRAILER PLATES

COMMERCIAL VEHICLE

TRUCK/ TRACTOR

APPORTIONED TRUCK

PLATE VALIDATION

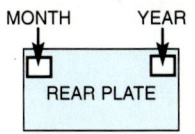

MONTH YEAR

REAR PLATE

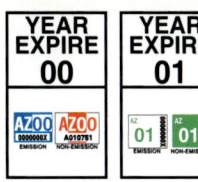

YEAR EXPIRE **00**

YEAR EXPIRE **01**

www.dot.state.az.us

"The Grand Canyon State" now issues only one reflectorized graphic license plate for most vehicles, having dropped the two-plate requirement. Plates continued to be issued in pairs for: Collegiate, Medal of Honor, POW, Pearl Harbor Survivors, Antique, Purple Heart. A new graphic base is being phased-in beginning on October 1, 1996 which will eventually replace all white-on-maroon plates.

Distinctive captions:

CLASSIC CAR - Vehicle listed by Classic Car Association of America
HISTORIC VEHICLE - A collectors vehicle at least 25 years old
HORSELESS CARRIAGE - A vehicle manufactured 1915 or earlier

Codes:

Arizona issues 3 alpha-3 numeric, and 3 numeric-3 alpha character plates to regular passenger vehicles. This numbering system is used for individual vehicle identification only, and does not contain any county of origin, occupation or other hidden codes. Only 1 plate is now required to be displayed, although earlier issues were in pairs.

Commercial vehicle plates have 6 characters:

1 **AB** -123 1 numeric - 2 alpha - 3 numeric
1 **ZA** -123 Bus and taxi plates display **Z** in first alpha position
1 **XA** -123 Trucks operating interstate display **X** as first alpha
1 **TA** -123 Truck tractors display **T** as first alpha

Prefixes can also be used for identification on older issue plates:

A	Arizona State Univ.	**K**	Univ. of Arizona
AZ	Dept. of Public Safety	**ST / SA**	State of Arizona
DL	Automobile dealer	**TR**	Trailer dealer
E	Environmental	**V**	Northern Ariz. Univ
ED	School vehicle	**XP**	Transporter
H	Hearing impaired	**Z**	Proportional trailer

All other classes of Arizona plates are easily identified by captions that appear on the plate.

Arizona Department of Revenue, Division of Motor Vehicles
1801 West Jefferson, Phoenix, AZ 85007   Tel. 602-255-7011

ARKANSAS

POLICE PATCH

DRIVERS LICENSE

PASSENGER PLATES

PASSENGER

PASSENGER
OLDER ISSUE

PERSONALIZED

DISABLED

DISABLED
VETERAN

COLLEGE
ARKANSAS
STATE UNIV.

AMATEUR
RADIO

CITY/COUNTY
OWNED

RETIRED
MILITARY

PEARL
HARBOR
SURVIVOR

MEDAL OF
HONOR

ANTIQUE

TRUCK AND TRAILER PLATES

TRUCK

APPORTIONED
TRUCK

SEMI-TRAILER

APPORTIONED
SEMI-TRAILER

16

PLATE VALIDATION

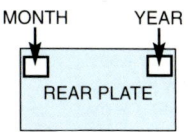

MONTH   YEAR

REAR PLATE

YEAR EXPIRE **00**

YEAR EXPIRE **01**

www.ahtd.state.ar.us/ahtdhtml

"The Natural State" issues one fully-reflectorized license plate for passenger vehicles. Many of the non-passenger and annual plates are not reflectorized.

Distinctive captions:

ARK NG--Arkansas National Guard
BS&O - Boy Scout and orphanage bus
BORDER CITY - Taxi licensed to operate in a limited area across state line
FARM PRODUCTS - Farm truck
FARM-TO-MARKET -Bus limited to operation between farm and market
PUBLIC PROPERTY - City or county-owned vehicle

Codes:

Passenger cars and pickup trucks are issued 3 alpha-3 numeric plates. Truck and trailer plates have 1 or 2 alpha prefix followed by numerics. The prefixes have the following meanings:

Passenger car:

DAV	Disabled veteran	**MX**	Manufacturer
EX	Extra dealer plate		(extra plate)
F	Franchise dealer	**POW**	Ex-POW
M	Master dealer	**PH**	Purple Heart
MF	Master Manufacturer	**PHS**	Pearl Harbor Survivor

Trucks and trailers:

B	Truck 6,001 - 20,000 lbs gross loaded weight
B over **T**	Boat trailer
G over **T**	Goose neck trailer
C	Truck 20,001 - 40,000 lbs gross loaded weight
D	Truck 40,001 - 56,000 lbs gross loaded weight
E	Truck 56,001 - 59,000 lbs gross loaded weight
H	Truck 60,001 - 68,000 lbs gross loaded weight
J	Truck 68,001 - 73,000 lbs gross loaded weight
K	Truck 73,281 - 87,000 lbs gross loaded weight
NR	Vehicle transporting natural resources (forest products, clay etc.)
ST	Semi-trailer
T	Full trailer
T over P	Transporter
X	County or city-owned truck

Arkansas Revenue Division Registration & Title Section
P.O. Box 1272, Little Rock, AR 72203   Tel. 501-682-4702

CALIFORNIA

POLICE PATCH

DRIVERS LICENSE

PASSENGER PLATES

PASSENGER
BASE

PASSENGER
BASE 1988
ISSUE

PASSENGER
BASE 1987
ISSUE

PASSENGER
BASE 1970
ISSUE

PASSENGER
BASE 1963
ISSUE

PERSONALIZED

CITY/COUNTY
OWNED

YOSEMITE
FOUNDATION

COLLEGIATE
UCLA

LAKE TAHOE

SAVE THE
COAST

ARTS

TRUCK AND TRAILER PLATES

COMMERICAL
VEHICLE
TRUCK OR
TRAILER

APPORTIONED
VEHICLE

COMMERCIAL
VEHICLE
TRUCK OR
TRAILER

COMMERCIAL
VEHICLE
TRUCK OR
TRAILER

PLATE VALIDATION

MONTH   YEAR

YEAR EXPIRE 00	YEAR EXPIRE 01	**CA**

FRONT PLATE   REAR PLATE

CA 2000 L 0000000M   CA 2001 L 0000000M   www.dmv.ca.gov

"The Golden State" has not had a complete general plate re-issue since 1963, and five different bases are currently in use. Plates are issued in pairs, and fully-reflectorized plates were first issued in 1982. Special plates to commemorate the 1984 Olympics and the U.S. Olympic Training Center have been issued and remain valid.

Distinctive captions:

DISMANTLER- Plate to move a vehicle to a place of dismantling (junkyard)
HISTORICAL- A vehicle manufactured after 1922 and at least 25 years old
HORSELESS CARRIAGE- 16- cyl. engine pre-1965, or vehicle mfg. before 1923

 Exempt State

 Exempt City (county gov't. special districts)

 Press Photographer

Codes:

California issues 6 character (3 alpha-3 numeric; 3 numeric -3 alpha) and 7character (1 numeric-3 alpha-3 numeric plates. Several graphic design base plates are in use. Commercial vehicle plates have 1 alpha-6 numeric plates where the alpha appears in different positions.

The following alpha prefixes are reserved for special groups:

A- State Assemblyman
AR- Assemblyman retired
AP,AT,BT,CT,DT,FT,GT-Apportioned
AA-TZ- Trailer not subject to wgt.fee
DP - Disabled person
DV - Disabled veteran
DSM- Dismantler
DST- Distributor
MFG - Manufacturer

POW- Prisoner of War
RMF - Remanufacturer
S- State senator
SR- Retired senator
SE - Special Equipment
TRN - Transporter
ZZ - Permanent trailer fleet
   "C"- denotes Jartran, Inc.
   "D" - denotes U-Haul Co.

California does not indicate county of origin or weight of vehicle on plates. California old car enthusiasts are able to register their 1962 or earlier vehicles with a matched pair of original California plates of the year the vehicle was manufactured.

California Department of Motor Vehicles
2415 First Avenue, Sacramento, CA 95818   Tel. 916-657-7677

COLORADO

POLICE PATCH

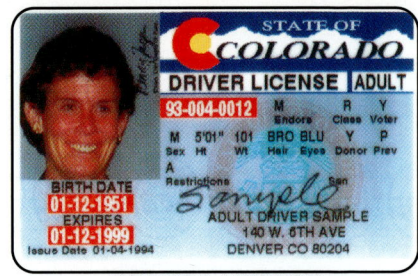

DRIVERS LICENSE

PASSENGER PLATES

NEW PLATE
SCHEDULED
JANUARY 2000

PASSENGER
OLDER BASE

PASSENGER
OLDER BASE

PERSONALIZED

DENIM
PLATE

DISABLED

CITY OWNED

COUNTY
OWNED

MEMBER OF
CONGRESS

FORMER POW

PEARL HAR-
BOR SURVIVOR

COLLECTOR

TRUCK AND TRAILER PLATES

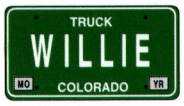

PERSONALIZED
TRUCK

APPORTIONED
TRUCK

GVW TRUCK

PERMANENT
TRAILER

PLATE VALIDATION

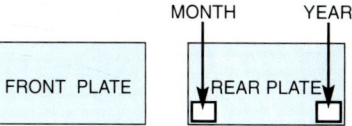

MONTH   YEAR

FRONT PLATE   REAR PLATE

www.state.co.us

Colorado issues two partially-reflectorized (glass beads on paint) white on green plates. These plates contain a county code numbering system. Colorful blue on white "designer" plates are available for an additional fee.

Distinctive captions:

COLLECTORS SERIES - Vehicle 25 years or older
DEPOT - Used by dealers to move a vehicle

Codes:

All private and commercial license plates have an alpha prefix that indicates the county of origin and (county seat) as follows:

previous	New code	County	County seat	previous	New code	County	County seat
AA-CV	AAA-DZZ	Denver	Denver	XP	UBL-UCA	Lincoln	Hugo
GP-HD	VEC-VVC	Pueblo	Pueblo	XS	EPB-EPU	Elbert	Kiowa
HY-JM	WAA-WNK	Weld	Greeley	XU	VYP-VZA	Saguache	Saguache
JX-LL	KAA-LZZ	El Paso	Colo. Springs	XW	EET-EFA	Crowley	Ordway
FR-FT,FV		El Paso	Colo. Springs	XY-XZ	VBB-VBR	Phillips	Holyoke
LM-LN	UAA-UBK	Las Animas	Trinidad	YA-YA	EEL-EES	Costilla	San Luis
LU-MK	FHA-FZZ	Larimer	Ft. Collins	YB	WNL-WNY	Sedgwick	Julesburg
FX-FY		Larimer	Ft. Collins	YD-YE	EYC-EZC	Gunnison	Gunnison
ML-NF	MAA-NZZ	Boulder	Boulder	YF-YG	FCD-FDE	Lake	Leadville
FH-FP		Boulder	Boulder	YJ-YK	UNS-UPX	Moffat	Craig
NG-NT	UEJ-UNL	Mesa	Grand Junction	YL-YL	WRN-WSR	Teller	Cripple Creek
PA-PC	UXS-UZZ	Otero	LaJunta	YM-YN,ZT	EMB-EPA	Eagle	Eagle
PH-RP	PAA-RZZ	Arapahoe	Littleton	YP-YP	WUS-WUY	Kiowa	Eads
FA-FG		Arapahoe	Littleton	YR-YR	ECM-ECT	Cheyenne	Cheyenne Wells
RS-TD	GAA-JZZ	Jefferson	Golden	YS-YT	EHW-EMA	Douglas	Castle Rock
HG-HW		Jefferson	Golden	YU-YU	FAA-FAL	Archuleta	Pagosa Springs
TE-UF	SAA-TZZ	Adams	Brighton	YV	VVD-VVV	Rio Blanco	Meeker
GA-GG		Adams	Brighton	YX-YX	VZF-VZR	San Miguel	Telluride
UG-UJ	UCB-UEH	Logan	Sterling	YY-YZ	ECU-EDU	Clear Creek	Georgetown
UP-UT	EPV-ETV	Fremont	Canon City	ZA-ZA	EFB-EFG	Custer	Westcliffe
UW-UY	UVA-UXR	Morgan	Ft. Morgan	ZB-ZC	EWZ-EYB	Grand	Hot Sulfur Spgs.
VE	EZF-EZW	Huerfano	Walsenburg	ZD-ZD	VAH-VBA	Park	Fairplay
VG-VH	VDN-VEY	Prowers	Lamar	ZE-ZE	VZB-VZE	San Juan	Silverton
VL-VN	EFH-EHP	Delta	Delta	ZF-ZF	VAA-VAG	Ouray	Ouray
VS-VT	WTL-WUR	Yuma	Wray	ZG-ZP	VBS-VDM	Pitkin	Aspen
VV-VY	FDF-FGB	La Plata	Durango	ZH-ZH	EHR-EHV	Dolores	Dove Creek
WB-WD	USM-UUZ	Montrose	Montrose	ZJ-ZJ	FGC-FGH	Jackson	Walden
WG	EBE-EBW	Baca	Springfield	ZK-ZK	EWN-EWV	Gilpin	Central City
WJ-WK	VVW-VWZ	Rio Grande	Del Norte	ZL,ZR	WNZ-WRM	Summit	Breckenridge
WM-WR	ETW-ETM	Garfield	Glenwood Spgs.	ZM-ZM	UNM-UNR	Mineral	Creede
WS	EDV-EEK	Conejos	Conejos	ZN-ZN	EZD-EZE	Hinsdale	Lake City
WU-WV	WUZ-WVV	Kit Carson	Burlington				
WW	WST-WTK	Washington	Akron				
WZ-XA	VXA-VYN	Routt	Steamboat Spgs.				
XC	EBX-ECL	Bent	Las Animas				
XE-XF	EAA-EBD	Alamosa	Alamosa				
XH-XJ	FAM-FCC	Chaffee	Salida				
XL-XM	UPY-USL	Montezuma	Cortez				

Other codes:
ABC- Always Buy Colorado (products)
CC - Honorary Consul
MC - Member of Congress
SMM - Special mobile equipment
USS - U.S.Senator
ZAA-ZZZ - Rental cars

CONNECTICUT

POLICE PATCH

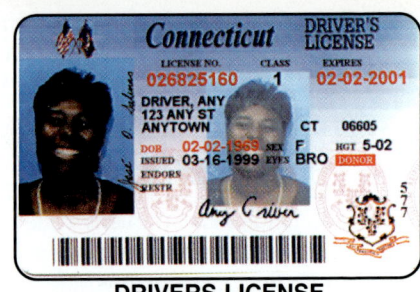

DRIVERS LICENSE

PASSENGER PLATES

PASSENGER
BASE

PASSENGER
OLDER BASE

PERSONALIZED

ENVIRONMENT

DISABLED

STATE OWNED
PREFIXED IS
DEPT. CODE

COLLEGIATE
UNIV. OF CONN

ENVIRONMENT

PETS

SCHOOL BUS

COLLECTOR

NEW YORK
PRESS

TRUCK AND TRAILER PLATES

APPORTIONED
TRUCK

COMBINATION
PRIVATE AND
COMMERCIAL

TRUCK

APPORTIONED
TRAILER

PLATE VALIDATION

MO/YR

YEAR EXPIRE 00	YEAR EXPIRE 01
APR 2000 CT0000443	JAN 2001 CT0044491

www.state.ct.us/dot

FRONT PLATE	REAR PLATE

"The Constitution State" issues two partially-reflectorized (glass beads on paint) license plates. Some special plates are now fully-reflectorized.

Distinctive captions:

CONSTITUTION STATE - Connecticut's colonial government served as a model for the U.S. Constitution

COMBINATION - Vehicle used for both private and commercial purposes

EXP TEST- Plate used to test experimental vehicles

FARM - Vehicle transporting farm prod. or livestock; limited highway use

LIVERY - Passenger vehicle for hire (other than taxi or bus)

REPAIR - Plate issued to persons engaged in motor vehicle repair

SERV. BUS - Vehicle used to transport 8 or more people without charge

TRANS.- Transporter plate

VETERAN- Disabled veteran

VAN POOL- Commuter van

Codes:

Most Connecticut passenger plates have 3 numeric - 3 alpha characters. However, since 1957-74 white on blue, 1974-76 blue on white, 1976-87 slogan blue and 1988 map blue plates are still in use. Various alpha/numeric configurations can be observed.

Commercial vehicle plates have 1 alpha-5 numeric characters. The following alpha characters are reserved for special use:

A- Apportioned
AT- Apportioned truck
AL- American Legion
ARC- American Red Cross
CNP- Conn. news photographer

DA - DZ - Used car dealer
DV - Disabled veteran
MD - Medical doctor
NYP - New York Press
RA - RZ - Repair
SX - Special dealer

U - Hearse
VFW -Veterans' organization
XA-XZ- New car dealer
YD - Yankee Division

License plates are revalidated every two years by a decal. The schedule is based on the first letter of the owner's last name.

INITIAL	RENEWAL MO.	INITIAL	RENEWAL MO.	
A-B	MAY	**M-O**	NOVEMBER	COMMERCIAL- April
C	JUNE	**P-R**	DECEMBER	COMBINATION - July
D-F	AUGUST	**S**	JANUARY	MISCELLANEOUS - March
G-J	SEPTEMBER	**T-Z**	FEBRUARY	
K,L,N	OCTOBER			

The alpha suffix on municipal plates is the initials of the city or town. Plate numbers:1 - 5,000 are assigned by the Commissioner of Motor Vehicles. Connecticut does not indicate the county of origin or weight of a vehicle on the plate.

Connecticut Department of Motor Vehicles
60 State Street, Wethersfield, CT 06109-1896   Tel. 860- 566- 2240

DELAWARE

POLICE PATCH

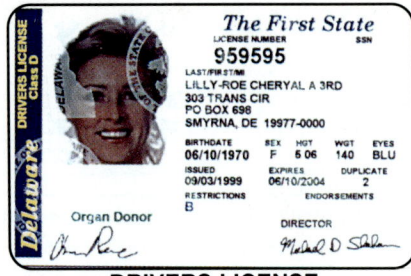

DRIVERS LICENSE

PASSENGER PLATES

PASSENGER
BASE

PERSONALIZED

OPTIONAL
PORCELAIN

OPTIONAL
GRAPHIC

SUPPORT
WILDLIFE

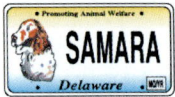

ANIMAL
FRIENDLY

STATE
SENATOR

JUDGE

LIONS CLUB

RETIRED
MILITARY

SORORITY

PLEASURE AND
COMMERCIAL
USE

TRUCK AND TRAILER PLATES

COMMERCIAL

TRAILER

APPORTIONED
TRUCK

APPORTIONED
TRAILER

24

PLATE VALIDATION

MO/YR

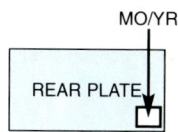
REAR PLATE

YEAR EXPIRE 00

YEAR EXPIRE 01

www.state.de.us/deidot/index

"The First State" issues one fully-reflectorized license plate for all vehicles. Delaware's plates are unique because they are neither embossed or debossed. They are made with a silk-screening process and are completely flat. Passenger vehicle plates are all numeric.

Distinctive captions:

THE FIRST STATE- Delaware was the first state to ratify the Constitution
STREET ROD - Modified antique vehicle manufactured prior to 1949

Codes:

Delaware does not designate county of origin or weight of a vehicle on license plates. Regular passenger plates are all numeric. Alpha prefixes indicate classes of vehicles as follows:

A	Ambulance	**MC**	Motorcycle
C	Commercial vehicle	**MIA**	Missing in action
CL	Commercial vehicle	**MOP**	Moped
CT	Contractor	**N over G**	National Guard
D	Dealer	**P over C**	Pleasure -commercial
DAV	Disabled veteran	**POW**	Former prisoner of war
DU	Ducks Unlimited	**R**	Rescue vehicle
F	Farm Implement	**RF**	Armed forces reserves
FD	Fire Dept	**RV**	Recreational vehicle
FOP	Frat. order of police	**SP**	Retired State Police
FT	Farm truck	**T**	Trailer
HP	Handicapped	**TC**	Tow car
L over A	Ladies Auxiliary	**V over F**	Volunteer Firefighter
LE	Del. Corr. Officers Assn.		

Delaware permits low number (passenger plate under 87,000 and commercial plates C-1 to C-9999) porcelain plates can be re-manufactured in black and white for use on any passenger or commercial vehicle (except PC plates). They must display a current validation decal.

Apportioned vehicles are issued plates prefixed with: C and CL.

DISTRICT OF COLUMBIA

POLICE PATCH

DRIVERS LICENSE

PASSENGER PLATES

PASSENGER BASE

HANDICAPPED

BICENTENNIAL

DISABLED VETERAN

U.S. GOVERNMENT

CITY COUNCIL

INNAUGURAL PLATE

CLERGY

ANTIQUE CAR

RENTAL

TAXI

DEALER

TRUCK AND TRAILER PLATES

APPORTIONED

COMMERCIAL

TRAILER

PLATE VALIDATION

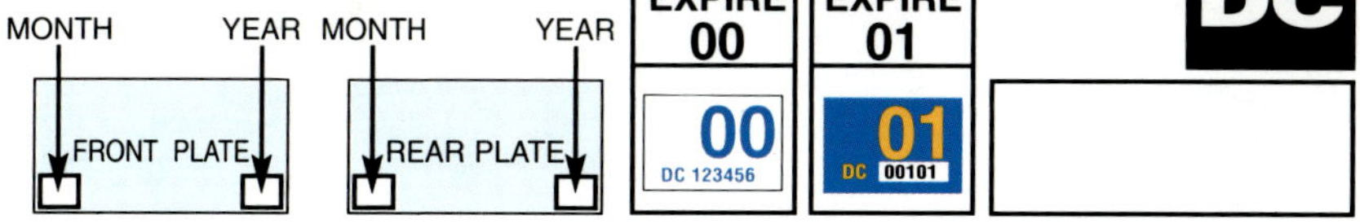

MONTH   YEAR   MONTH   YEAR

↓ FRONT PLATE ↓   ↓ REAR PLATE ↓

YEAR EXPIRE 00	YEAR EXPIRE 01
00 DC 123456	01 DC 00101

DC

The "Capital City" issues two fully-reflectorized red, white and blue license plates. Low number plates (1 -1250) are assigned annually by the mayor's office.

Distinctive captions:

All words embossed or screen-printed on District of Columbia plates are self-explanatory.

Codes:

Regular passenger vehicle license plates have 6 numeric characters. Trucks, trailers, and bus plates have an alpha prefix followed by numerics. The following alpha prefixes have special meaning:

B- Bus
C- Commercial vehicle
CL- Clergy
D- Dealer
DAV- Disabled veteran
GVT- District of Columbia Govt.
GW- George Wash. Univ.
HMV- Historic motor vehicle
H- Taxi for hire

H over **P**- Handicapped person
L- Limousine, livery
MD- Medical doctor
PHA-Prince Hall Mason
QUE - Omega Psi Phi Frat.
R- Rental vehicle
T- Trailer
TRP- Transporter

    District of Columbia does not indicate the weight class or use restrictions of a vehicle on the license plate.

D.C. Bureau of Motor Vehicle Services
301 C Street, NW, Washington, DC 20001   Tel. 202-727-1159

FLORIDA

POLICE PATCH

DRIVERS LICENSE

PASSENGER PLATES

PASSENGER
BASE

PASSENGER
OLDER BASE

PASSENGER
OLDER BASE

CHALLENGER

NEW
CHALLENGER

CONSERVE
WILDLIFE

STATE OWNED

COLLEGIATE
A&M

COLLEGIATE
BARRY UNIV.

COLLEGIATE
GATORS

PROTECT THE
MANATEE

PROTECT THE
PANTHER

SPECIAL
OLYMPICS

SUPPORT
EDUCATION

EVERGLADES

FISHING

TRUCK AND TRAILER PLATES

APPORTIONED
2000 EXPIRE

APPORTIONED
1999 EXPIRE

TRUCK &
TRAILERS
INTRA-STATE
USE

TRAILERS
PERMANENT
PLATE

28

PLATE VALIDATION

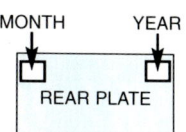

MONTH   YEAR

REAR PLATE

YEAR EXPIRE 00

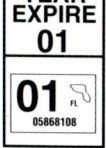

YEAR EXPIRE 01

www.hsmv.state.fl.us

"The Sunshine State" issues one fully-reflectorized license plate. All regular passenger plates display the county name (unless county officials request that "Sunshine State" be embossed instead). Florida has demonstrated that special license plates can be an excellent fund raising source having raised millions to: save the Manatee, Florida Panther and memorialize the Challenger, as well as to promote other causes.

Distinctive captions:

HORSELESS CARRIAGE - An exhibition vehicle 35 years old
INDEFINITE - Permanent rental trailer registration
REG ONLY- Vehicles with titles held by out-of-state finance companies
STREET ROD - Pre-1949 modified exhibit vehicle
RESTRICTED- Vehicles with restricted range of operation- Tow truck, hearse etc.

Codes:

The Florida numbering system is as follows:
Previous passenger, motor coach, light trucks: 3 alpha - 3 numeric and 4 alpha- 2 numeric. Currently it is 3 alpha - 2 numeric -1 alpha (ABC-12A).
Trucks, tractors and ambulances always have 6 characters: 1 or 2 alpha prefix- numerics
1 alpha suffix.

The letter "O" does not appear in the third position on passenger plates or the second alpha position on non-passenger plates. Numerics begin with 001, 0001, and 00001.

The county of origin appears at the bottom of all plates issued since 1980, except for permanent plates. DMV indicates Division of Motor Vehicles and is used instead of the county name on special plates. Counties may decide to use "Sunshine State" in lieu of county name

The following prefixes are reserved for special use:

ACS - Agriculture Consumer Svcs.
DC - Dept. of Corrections
DDL- Div. of Drivers Licensing
DMV - Div. of Motor Vehicles
DNR - Div. Natural Resources
DOT - Dept.. of Transportation
DV - Disabled Veteran
FBC - Florida Board of Conservation
FDC - Florida Dept. of Commerce
FFS - Florida Forest Service
FHP- Florida Highway Patrol
FIC - Florida Industrial Commission
FMP - Florida Marine Patrol

FPS - Florida Park Service
GFC - Game and Fish Commission
HP- Handicapped person
M plus 2 alphas- Dealers
MC - Member of Congress
MF- Franchised vehicle dealer
PP - Harvest truck
PRESS - Members of the press
PSC - Public Service Commission
USS - U.S. Senator
X - Exempt from registration fee

Florida Department of Highway Safety & Motor Vehicles
Neil Kirkman Building, 2900 Apalachee Parkway , Tallahassee, FL 32399
Tel. 904-922-9000

GEORGIA

POLICE PATCH

DRIVERS LICENSE

PASSENGER PLATES

PASSENGER
1 PLATE, 1 DECAL

PERSONALIZED

HANDICAPPED

SHERIFF

COLLEGIATE GEORGIA TECH.

CONGRESSMAN

STATE REPRESENTATIVE

FOREIGN GOVERNMENT

SPECIAL OLYMPICS

RESERVE

HONORARY CONSUL

NATIONAL GUARD

TRUCK AND TRAILER PLATES

APPORTIONED EXPIRE 2000

TRAILER PERMANENT

TRUCK

APPORTIONED EXPIRE 1998

PLATE VALIDATION

MO/YR

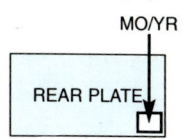

REAR PLATE

YEAR EXPIRE 00	YEAR EXPIRE 01	
		 www.ga.us.department/dor

The "Peach State" issues one fully-reflectorized license plate with a uniform format and color scheme for each vehicle. A new graphic general issue is being phased-in during 1997 and will replace all 1990 base plates. Passenger plates display the county name on a decal.

Distinctive captions:

HISTORICAL VEHICLE- Vehicle at least 30 years old
LIMITED - Bus operating to and from a military reservation
50 MILE- Bus limited to 50 mile operating radius
UNL- Unlimited bus licensed to operate throughout state

Codes:

Georgia issues passenger plates in a 3 numeric -3 alpha semi-permanent (7 year) cycle.The county of origin appears on the bottom of the plate.

Trucks and truck tractor plates have a 2 alpha weight class code prefix followed by numerics. Vehicles up to 26,000 lbs. gross weight receive 5 year plates. Vehicles over 26,000 lbs. are registered as intrastate Georgia, and interstate operation under the IRP. Intrastate vehicles are registered with annual plates and color combinations change yearly.

The prefixes are as follows:

AA-BZ	Auto and house trailers less than 1000 lbs. and all farm trailers
CA-CZ	Auto and house trailers more than 1000 lbs.
EA, FA, FB	Forest products truck
HB	Hearse and ambulances
HF	Trucks and tractors for hire 26,001 - 30,000 lbs.
HG	Truck and truck tractors for hire 30,001 - 36,000 lbs.
HH	Trucks and truck tractors for hire 36,001 - 44,000 lbs.
HI	Trucks and tractors for hire 44,001 - 54,999 lbs.
HJ	Trucks and tractors for hire 55,000 - 63,280 lbs.
HK	Trucks and tractors for hire 63,281 - maximum wgt.
JA- JM	Trucks and tractors 14,001 - 18,000 lbs.
JN- JZ	Trucks and tractors 18,001 - 26,000 lbs.
PF	Trucks and tractors not for hire 26,001 - 30,000 lbs.
PG	Trucks and tractors not for hire 30,001 - 36,000 lbs.
PH	Trucks and tractors not for hire 36,000 - 44,000 lbs.
PI	Trucks and tractors not for hire 44,001 - 54,999 lbs.
PJ	Trucks and tractors not for hire 55,000 - 63,280 lbs.
PK	Trucks and tractors not for hire 63,280 - maximum wgt.
QA- TZ	Trucks and tractors and farm trucks less than 6,000 lbs.
WA- WZ	Trucks and tractors and farm trucks 6,001 - 10,000 lbs.
XA	Trucks and tractors and farm trucks 10,001 - 14,000 lbs.

Georgia Department of Revenue Motor Vehicle Division
1200 Tradeport Boulevard, Hapeville, GA 30354   Tel. 404-362-6463

HAWAII

POLICE PATCH

DRIVERS LICENSE

PASSENGER PLATES

PASSENGER
2 PLATES, 1
DECAL ON
REAR

PERSONALIZED

VETERAN

PEARL
HARBOR
SURVIVOR

PURPLE HEART

CITY/COUNTY
OWNED

STATE VEHICLE

WAGON HORSE
DRAWN
VEHICLE

COLLECTOR

TRUCK AND TRAILER PLATES

TRUCK

FLEET VEHICLE

PLATE VALIDATION

MO/YR

| FRONT PLATE | REAR PLATE | YEAR EXPIRE **00** MAY 2000 A 000000 | YEAR EXPIRE **01** MAY 2001 A 000000 | www.hawaii.gov/dot |

The "Aloha State" issues two fully-reflectorized license plates. A county code is used in the numbering system.

Distinctive captions:

ALOHA STATE - Aloha is the Hawaiian word of greeting
FLEET - Used by companies that operate fleets of vehicles
HORSELESS CARRIAGE - Antique vehicle
WAGON - Horse-drawn vehicle

Codes:

Passenger vehicles are 3 alpha - 3 numeric.
  The following alpha prefixes indicate county of origin:

AAA - BZZ City and county of Honolulu (Oahu)
HAA - HZZ County of Hawaii (Island of Hawaii)
MAA - MZZ County of Maui (Islands of Maui, Molokai, Lanai)
KAA - KZZ County of Kauai (Island of Kauai)

The following prefixes are reserved for:

BUS - Honolulu municipal bus
BWS - Honolulu Board of Water Supply
C&C - City and County Honolulu
C of H - County of Hawaii
C of K- County of Kauai
C of M - County of Maui

CJ - Chief Justice St. Supreme Court
HFD - Both Hawaii and Honolulu Fire
HPD - Honolulu Police Dept
KFD - Kauai Fire Dept
MFD - Maui Fire Dept
P - Fleet vehicle

Truck and trailer plates are the same design as passenger plates.
The characters are reversed 3 numeric - 3 alpha.
  The first alpha on truck and trailer plates is a county code:

H	County of Hawaii
M	County of Maui
K	County of Kauai
T	City & County of Honolulu truck
W	City & County of Honolulu trailer

Hawaii Motor Vehicle Safety Office, City & County of Honolulu
P.O. Box 30300, Honolulu, HI 96820-0330   Tel. 808-532-4325

IDAHO

POLICE PATCH

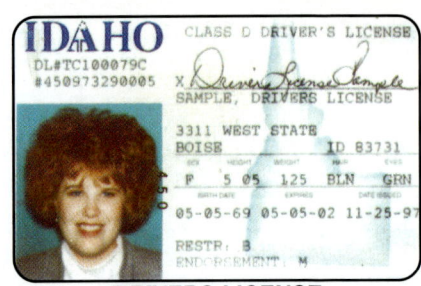

DRIVERS LICENSE

PASSENGER PLATES

PASSENGER
2 PLATES 1 DECAL

PERSONALIZED

**WILDLIFE
CONSERVATION**

**WILDLIFE
CONSERVATION**

CONSERVATION

HANDICAPPED

**NATIONAL
GUARD**

LEGISLATIVE

STREET ROD

**COLLEGIATE
BOISE STATE**

SNOWMOBILE

STATE POLICE

TRUCK AND TRAILER PLATES

COMMERCIAL

APPORTIONED

PLATE VALIDATION

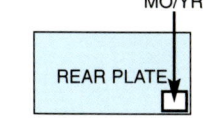

MO/YR

YEAR EXPIRE 00	YEAR EXPIRE 01

FRONT PLATE | REAR PLATE | www.state.id.us/itd/dmv

The "Gem State" home of "Famous Potatoes" issues two fully-reflectorized license plates with a unique county code system. Counties are coded alphabetically; the tenth county starting with "B" receives a "10 B" prefix.

Distinctive captions:

CLASSIC- Vehicle over 30 years old used for exhibition
LOANER- Used on dealer vehicles loaned to customers
STREET ROD- Modified vehicle manufactured prior to 1949

Codes:

Passenger vehicles and light trucks are issued plates with an alpha/numeric prefix which indicates the county of origin

The county (county seat) codes are as follows:

1A	Ada (Boise)	4C	Cassia (Burley)	4L	Lincoln (Shoshone)
2A	Adams (Council)	5C	Clark (Dubois)	1M	Madison
1B	Bannock (Pocatello)	6C	Clearwater (Orofino)		(Rexburg)
2B	Bear Lake (Paris)	7C	Custer (Challis)	2M	Minidoka (Rupert)
3B	Benewah (StMaries)	E	Elmore (Mtn. Home)	N	Nez Perce
4B	Bingham (Blackfoot)	1F	Franklin (Preston)		(Lewiston)
5B	Blaine (Hailey)	2F	Fremont	10	Oneida (Malad City)
6B	Boise (Idaho City)		(St. Anthony)	20	Owyhee (Murphy)
7B	Bonner (Sandpoint)	1G	Gem (Emmett)	1P	Payette (Payette)
8B	Bonneville	2G	Gooding (Gooding)	2P	Power
	(Idaho Falls)	I	Idaho (Grangeville)		(American Falls)
9B	Boundary	1J	Jefferson (Rigby)	S	Shoshone (Wallace)
	(Bonners Ferry)	2J	Jerome (Jerome)	1T	Teton (Driggs)
10B	Butte (Arco)	K	Kootenai	2T	Twin Falls
1C	Camas (Fairfield)		(Coeur d'Alene)		(Twin Falls)
2C	Canyon (Caldwell)	1L	Latah (Moscow)	V	Valley (Cascade)
3C	Caribou	2L	Lemhi (Salmon)	W	Washington
	(Soda Springs)	3L	Lewis (Nez Perce)		(Weiser)

Alpha prefixes and suffixes reserved for special use:

DLR	Dealer	**LAA-LAZ**	Loaner	**PRP**	Apportioned
DV	Disabled Veteran	**LTD**	Full fee limited	**RPO**	Repossession
ISP	Idaho St. Police	**MAA-MZZ**	Motorcycle	**UAA- UZZ**	Utility trailer

Idaho does not designate the weight of a vehicle on the plate.
Letters I,O,Q are not used as alpha characters on Idaho plates.

Idaho Transportation Department, Motor Vehicle Division
3311 West State Street, P.O. Box 7129, Boise, ID 83707-1129   Tel. 208-334-8000

ILLINOIS

POLICE PATCH

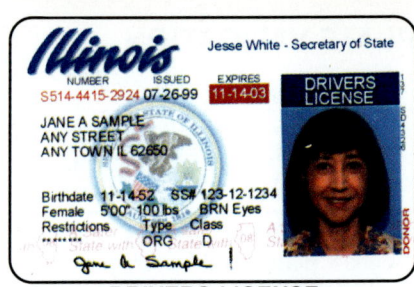

DRIVERS LICENSE

PASSENGER PLATES

PASSENGER
2 PLATES 1
DECAL ON
REAR

PERSONALIZED

ENVIRONMENT

PREVENT
VIOLENCE

ELECTED
OFFICIAL

STATE OWNED

DISABLED
VETERAN

MILITARY
RESERVE

NATIONAL
GUARD

FIRE FIGHTER

SPORTING

SPECIAL
EVENT

TRUCK AND TRAILER PLATES

APPORTIONED

TRUCK

APPORTIONED
TRAILER

LIGHT TRUCK

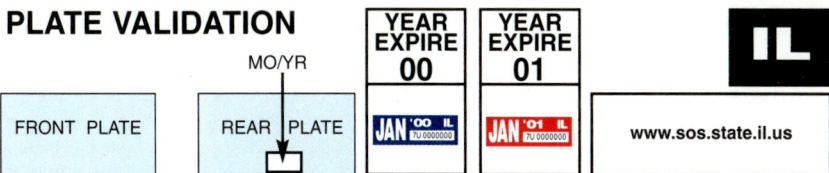

PLATE VALIDATION

MO/YR

FRONT PLATE

REAR PLATE

YEAR EXPIRE 00

YEAR EXPIRE 01

JAN '00 IL 7U 0000000

JAN '01 IL 7U 0000000

IL

www.sos.state.il.us

The "Land of Lincoln" issues two fully-reflectorized license plates. Illinois which produces more varieties of plates than any other state, issues a large number of annual (fiscal year) plates for non-passenger vehicles, and over 100 different special-event plates valid for only a 60 day period.

Distinctive captions:

CEREMONIAL - Parade vehicle
LIVERY- Vehicle for hire
REPOSSESSOR - Used to repossess motor vehicles

Codes:

Passenger plates are issued for the calendar year and are:
all numeric,1 alpha- 5 numeric, 2 alpha-4 numeric, 3 alpha-3 numeric, 3 alpha- 4 numeric

Prefixes reserved for special groups and vehicle classifications:

A over **V**	Antique vehicle	**M**	County, municipal
DAV	Disabled Veteran	**MFR**	Vehicle manufacturer
D over **L**	Dealer	**TX**	Taxi-cab
F H	Funeral home	**U**	State-owned vehicle
I over **T**	Transporter plate	**CV** (suffix)	Charitable vehicle

Trucks and other commercial vehicles operating intrastate (only within Illinois) receive plates by the fiscal year July - June. Trucks operating interstate are issued prorated or apportioned plates on a calendar basis Jan.-Dec. The numeric characters on these plates are solely for individual vehicle identification. The last (or bottom) alpha character is a weight code:

TRUCKS

Suffix	Gross weight (lbs)
B	8,000 lbs. or less
D	8,001 - 12,000
F	12,001 - 16,000
H	16,001 - 24,000
J	24,001 -28,000
K	28,001 - 32,000
N	32,001 - 41,000
P	41,001 - 45,000
R	45,001 - 50,000
S	50,001 - 59,500
T	59,501 - 64,000

Suffix	Gross weight (lbs)
V	64,001 -73,280
X	73,281 -77,000
Z	77,001 -80,000

TRAILERS

T over A	3,000 lbs. or less
B over A	3,001 - 8,000
C over A	8,001 - 10,000
E over A	10,001 - 14,000
G over A	14,001 - 20,000
K over A	20,001 - 32,000
L over A	32,001 - 36,00
N over A	36,001 - 40,000

BM - Municipal bus
CR - Ceremonial
CM - Commuter van
CN - Conservation

EL - Electric vehicle
FM - Farm machinery
FS - Fertilizer spreader
MC - Medicar

PM - Permanent equip.
PT - Public transportation
S over **T**- Semi trailer
T over second alpha- full trailer

Illinois Secretary of State's Office, Vehicle Services Department
Room 312, Howlett Building, 501 South Second Street, Springfield, IL 62756
Tel. 217-785-3000

INDIANA

POLICE PATCH

DRIVERS LICENSE

PASSENGER PLATES

**PASSENGER
1 PLATE 2
DECALS**

PERSONALIZED

ENVIRONMENT

**CHILDRENS
TRUST**

EDUCATION

**ELECTED
STATE
OFFICIAL**

MUNICIPAL

PURPLE HEART

COLLECTOR

CONGRESSMAN

REPRESENTATIVE

PERSONALIZED

TRUCK AND TRAILER PLATES

APPORTIONED

**SEMI-TRAILER
PERMANENT**

**TRAILER
APPORTIONED**

TRUCK

PLATE VALIDATION

MONTH   YEAR

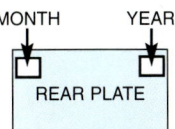

REAR PLATE

YEAR EXPIRE 00	YEAR EXPIRE 01
	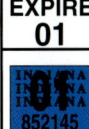

state in.us/bmvexpress

The home of "Amber Waves of Grain" issues one fully-reflectorized license plate. A county code system is used in the numeric prefix.

Distinctive captions:

HOUSE CAR - Vehicle one can live in;   SCHOOL T.C. - Driver training car

Codes:

Private passenger vehicles and light truck plates (pickups) have a numeric prefix that is a county code. The 1 alpha and 4 numeric characters that follow have no special significance other than identify the individual vehicle.

The county and (county seats) are as follows:

1. **Adams** (Decatur)
2. **Allen** (Ft. Wayne)
3. **Bartholomew** (Columbus)
4. **Benton** (Fowler)
5. **Blackford** (Hrtfrd Cty.)
6. **Boone** (Lebanon)
7. **Brown** (Nashville)
8. **Carroll**(Delphi)
9. **Cass**(Logansport)
10. **Clark** (Jeffersonville)
11. **Clay** (Brazil)
12. **Clinton** (Frankfort)
13. **Crawford** (English)
14. **Daviess** (Washngtn.)
15. **Dearborn** (Lwrncbrg)
16. **Decatur** (Grensbrg.)
17. **Dekalb** (Auburn)
18. **Delaware** (Muncie)
19. **Dubois** (Jasper)
20. **Elkhart** (Goshen)
21. **Fayette** (Connersville)
22. **Floyd** (New Albany)
23. **Fountain** (Covington)
24. **Franklin**(Brookville)

25. **Fulton** (Rochester)
26. **Gibson** (Princeton)
27. **Grant** (Marion)
28. **Greene** (Bloomfield)
29. **Hamilton** (Nobles-ville)
30. **Hancock** (Greenfld.)
31. **Harrison** (Corydon)
32. **Hendricks** (Dansville)
33. **Henry** (New Castle)
34. **Howard** (Kokomo)
35. **Huntingto** (Hntgtn.)
36. **Jackson** (Brwnstwn.)
37. **Jasper** (Rnsselaer.)
38 **Jay** (Portland)
39.**Jefferson** (Madison)
40. **Jennings**(Vernon)
41. **Johnson**(Franklin)
42. **Knox** (Vincennes)
43. **Kosciusko** (Warsaw)
44. **Lagrange**(Lagrange)
45. **Lake** (Crown Point)
46. **La Porte** (La Porte)
47. **Lawrence** (Bedford)
48. **Madiso**(Anderson)

49. **Marion**(Indianapolis)
50. **Marshall**(Plymouth)
51. **Martin** (Shoals)
52. **Miami** (Peru)
53. **Monroe** (Bloomngtn.)
54. **Montgomery** (Crawfordsville)
55. **Morgan** (Martinsville)
56. **Newton**(Kentland)
57. **Noble** (Albion)
58. **Ohio** (Rising Sun)
59. **Orange** (Paoli)
60. **Owen** (Spencer)
61. **Parke** (Rockville)
62. **Perry** (Cannelton)
63. **Pike** (Petersburg)
64. **Porter** (Valpariso)
65. **Posey** (Mt Vernon)
66. **Pulaski**(Winamac)
67.**Putnam**(Greencstle.)
68. **Randolph**(Winchstr.)
69. **Ripley** (Versailles)
70. **Rush** (Rushville)
71. **St.Joseph** (S. Bend)
72. **Scott** (Scottsburg)
73. **Shelby** (Shelbyville)
74.**Spencer** (Rockport)
75. **Starke** (Knox)
76. **Steuben** (Angola)

77.**Sullivan** (Sullivan)
78.**Switzerland** (Vevay)
79.**Tippecanoe**(Lafayette)
80.**Tipton** (Tipton)
81. **Union** (Liberty)
82. **Vanderburgh** (Evansville)
83. **Vermillion** (Newport)
84. **Vigo** (Terre Haute)
85. **Wabash** (Wabash)
86. **Warren** (Williamsport)
87. **Warrick** (Boonville)
88. **Washington** (Salem)
89. **Wayne**(Richmond)
90. **Wells** (Bluffton)
91. **White** (Monticello)
92.**Whitley** (Colmb.Cty.)
93. **Marion** (Indianapolis)
94. **Lake** (Crown Point)
95A. **Military& Special**
95B -Z. **Marion** (Indianapolis)
96. **Lake** (Crown Point)
97-99 **Marion** (Indianapolis)

Elected and appointed state officials have special plates captioned with a star. Low numbers are reserved for the following:

1 - Governor	5 - Treasurer	9- Clerk Supreme & Appellate Ct
2 - Lt. Governor	6 - Attorney General	10-14 - Supreme Court Justices
3 - Secretary of State	7 - Supt. of Schools	15 - 27 -Appellate Court Judges
4 - Auditor	8 - Recorder Supr. & Apel. Courts	

Truck, tractor and trailer plates are issued new every February. Instead of a county code, they contain a small numeric at the top of the plate that shows the weight class e.g. (26) indicates 26,000 to 36,000 lbs. gross vehicle weight.

Indiana Bureau of Motor Vehicles
100 North Senate # N 440, Indianapolis, IN 46204   Tel. 317-232-2798   **39**

IOWA

POLICE PATCH

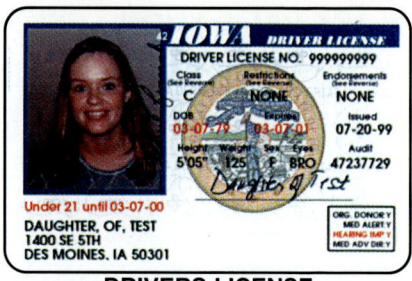

DRIVERS LICENSE

PASSENGER PLATES

PASSENGER
2 PLATES 1
DECAL

PERSONALIZED

DISABLED

DEALER

COLLEGIATE
CYCLONES

COLLEGIATE
HAWKEYES

PANTHERS

STATE OWNED

STATE POLICE

ENVIRONMENT

PURPLE HEART

CMH

TRUCK AND TRAILER PLATES

APPORTIONED
TRUCK

TRUCK

APPORTIONED
POWER UNIT

APPORTIONED
TRAILER

PLATE VALIDATION

MO/YR

FRONT PLATE

REAR PLATE

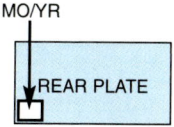

YEAR EXPIRE 00	YEAR EXPIRE 01

www.state.ia/us/
government/dot

The "Hawkeye State" is phasing-in a new graphic general issue base plate during 1997, which will replace all partially-reflectorized (glass beads on paint) plates. The county name appears on the bottom of new passenger and truck plates on a decal.

Distinctive captions:

SME - Special mobile equipment (construction equipment)
RESTRICTED - Nonstandard vehicle limited highway use
ANTIQUE - Motor vehicle at least 25 years old for limited use on highway
OFFICIAL SCHOOL - Owned by Iowa Independent School District

Codes:

Passenger vehicle plates display 3 alpha - 3 numeric characters. The county name appears on the lower center of the plate.

Trucks and commercial vehicle plates have the same design as passenger, however the characters are 2 alpha- 4 numeric. The following alpha characters are reserved for special use:

AA- Semi-trailer
AA- Travel trailer
AAA-2 plated vehicles
B- Bronze star
C Handicapped
D - Dealer
DV - Disabled veteran
E - Educational plate
KA - KZ - Truck, tractor full-year
F,FM- Firefighter
FF - Firefighter
LD - Urban transit bus
LF - LZ - Special mobile equipment

G- Pearl Harbor Survivor
H - Heritage plate
K- Kids plate
N - National Guard
PA- PZ - Apportioned truck full-year
P - Purple heart
RA- RZ - Apportioned trailer
SAA-SAZ - Special truck full-year
XX - Restricted vehicle
N - National guard
ZXY- Special plate.

Iowa Department of Transportation, Motor Vehicle Division
100 Euclid Avenue, P.O. Box 9278, Des Moines, IA 50306-9278   Tel. 515-237-3110

KANSAS

POLICE PATCH

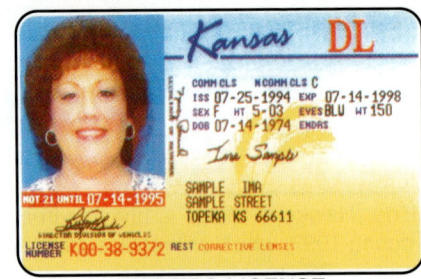

DRIVERS LICENSE

PASSENGER PLATES

PASSENGER 1 PLATE 2 DECALS

PERSONALIZED

HANDICAPPED

COLLEGIATE KANSAS STATE

HIGHWAY PATROL

COLLEGIATE KU

NATIONAL GUARD

FORMER POW

PURPLE HEART

STATE OWNED

AMATEUR RADIO

NEW PERSONALIZED

TRUCK AND TRAILER PLATES

PERMANENT APPORTIONED

TRUCK OR TRAILER

5 YEAR APPORTIONED TRAILER

PLATE VALIDATION

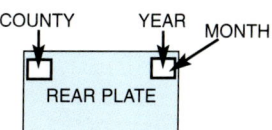

COUNTY   YEAR MONTH

REAR PLATE

YEAR EXPIRE **00**

AUTO **00** KANSAS 0000326

YEAR EXPIRE **01**

AUTO **01** KANSAS 0000326

www.ink.org/public/kdot

The "Sunflower State" issues one fully-reflectorized license plate, each containing a small two-letter county designation decal in an upper corner of the plate. Personalized plates are issued in pairs, and are a different graphic design.

Distinctive captions:

DRIVE AWAY - Drive-away operator other than dealer
FULL USE - Dealer plate that can be used on any vehicle
KCC - Kansas Commodity Commission plate issued to private carriers of commodities

Codes:

Kansas uses a 2 alpha county code on passenger plates. It appears on a decal on the upper left corner of the plate. The counties and (county seats) are as follows:

AL ALLEN (Iola)
AN ANDERSON (Garnett)
AT ATCHISON (Atchison)
AB BARBER (Medicine Lodge)
BT BARTON (Great Bend)
BB BOURBON (Ft. Scott)
BR BROWN (Hiawatha)
BU BUTLER (El Dorado)
CS CHASE (Ctnwood Falls)
CQ CHAUTAUQUA (Sedan)
CK CHEROKEE (Columbus)
CN CHEYENNE (St Francis)
CA CLARK (Ashland)
CY CLAY (Clay Center)
CD CLOUD (Concordia)
CF COFFEY (Burlington)
CM COMANCHE (Coldwtr.)
CL COWLEY (Winfield)
CR CRAWFORD (Girard)
DC DECATUR (Oberlin)
DK DICKINSON Abilene)
DP DONIPHAN(Troy)
DG DOUGLAS (Lawrence)
ED EDWARDS (Kinsley)
EK ELK (Howard)
EL ELLIS (Hays)
EW ELLSWORTH (Ellswrth)
FI FINNEY (Garden City)
FO FORD (Dodge City)
FR FRANKLIN (Ottawa)
GE GEARY (Junction City)
CO GOVE (Gove)
GH GRAHAM (Hill City)
GT GRANT (Ulysses)
GY GRAY (Cimarron)
GL GREELEY (Tribune)

GW GREENWOOD (Eureka)
HM HAMILTON (Syracuse)
HP HARPER (Anthony)
HV HARVEY (Newton)
HS HASKELL (Sublette)
HG HODGEMAN (Jetmore)
JA JACKSON (Holton)
JF JEFFERSON(Oskaloosa)
JW JEWELL (Mankato)
JO JOHNSON (Olathe)
KE KEARNY (Lakin)
KM KINGMAN (Kingman)
KW KIOWA (Greensburg)
LB LABETTE (Oswego)
LE LANE (Dighton)
LV LEAVENWORTH (Leavenworth)
LC LINCOLN (Lincoln)
LN LINN (Mound City)
LG LOGAN (Oakley)
LY LYON (Emporia)
MN MARION (Marion)
MS MARSHALL (Marysville)
MP McPHERSON (McPherson)
ME MEADE (Meade)
MI MIAMI (Paola)
MC MITCHELL (Beloit)
MG MONTGOMERY (Independence)
MR MORRIS (Council Grove)
MT MORTON (Elkhart)
NM NEMAHA (Seneca)
NO NEOSHO (Erie)
NS NESS (Ness City)
NT NORTON (Norton)
OS OSAGE (Lyndon)
OB OSBORNE (Osborne)

OT OTTAWA(Minneapolis)
PN PAWNEE (Larned)
PL PHILLIPS (Phillipsburg)
PT POTTAWATOMIE (Westmoreland)
PR PRATT (Pratt)
RA RAWLINS (Atwood)
RN RENO (Hutchinson)
RP REPUBLIC (Belleville)
RC RICE (Lyons)
RL RILEY (Manhattan)
RO ROOKS (Stockton)
RH RUSH (La Crosse)
RS RUSSELL (Russell)
SA SALINE (Salina)
SC SCOTT (Scott City)
SG SEDGWICK (Wichita)
SW SEWARD (Liberal)
SN SHAWNEE (Topeka)
SD SHERIDAN (Hoxie)
SH SHERMAN (Goodland)
SM SMITH (Smith Center)
SF STAFFORD (St John)
ST STANTON (Johnson)
SV STEVENS (Hugoton)
SU SUMNER (Wellington)
TH THOMAS (Colby)
TR TREGO (Wakeeney)
WB WABAUNSEE (Alma)
WA WALLACE (Sharon Springs)
WS WASHINGTON (Washington)
WH WICHITA (Leoti)
WL WILSON (Fredonia)
WO WOODSON (Yates Center)
WY WYANDOTTE (Kansas City)

The weight class of trucks and trailers is indicated by a decal on the plate.

Kansas Department of Revenue, Division of Motor Vehicles
Robert B. Docking Office Bldg. First Floor, Topeka, KS 66626-0001   Tel. 913-296-360143

KENTUCKY

POLICE PATCH

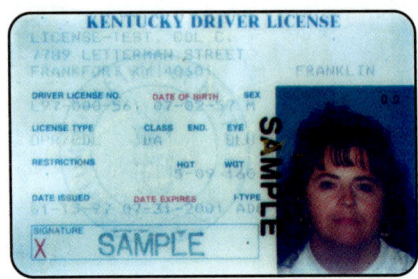

DRIVERS LICENSE

PASSENGER PLATES

PASSENGER
1 PLATE 1
DECAL

PERSONALIZED

HANDICAPPED

ENVIRONMENT

ENVIRONMENT

STATE POLICE

COLLEGIATE
UNIV. OF KY

CITY/COUNTY
OWNED

HORSEMAN
ASSOCIATION

PURPLE HEART

CARE ABOUT
KIDS

NATIONAL
GUARD

TRUCK AND TRAILER PLATES

APPORTIONED

TRUCK
LIMITED USE

PLATE VALIDATION

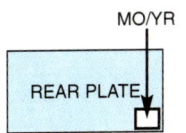

MO/YR

REAR PLATE

www.kytc.state.ky.us

The "Bluegrass State" issues one fully-reflectorized license plate for all passenger vehicles. A county name decal appears under the state name. Kentucky issues many annual non-passenger plates .

Distinctive captions:

HISTORIC - Vehicle at least 30 years old
JUDICIARY- Judge in the Kentucky judicial system
LIMITED - Truck that pays a limited registration fee. This includes vehicles hauling
        forest products, having a limited area of operations
PARKING - Special parking privileges for disabled persons
TRANSPORTATION - Kentucky Dept. of Transportation
TRUCK TRAILER - Semi-trailer

Codes:

Kentucky passenger vehicle plates have 3 alpha - 3 numeric characters and the county name appears at the top of the plate. The alpha numeric combinations are for individual vehicle identification only, there are no codes.
Official state owned vehicle plates usually begin with **K**, and there is no department or use numbering system.
County and city-owned vehicles usually begin with **L**. There is no other significance to the alpha numeric numbering system.
Owners of personalized plates receive new plates annually.
Truck plates have 2 alpha and 4 numerics that appear in various positions.
Truck plates do not indicate county of origin. Any special use, weight class and restrictions appear as captions on the plate.
Dealer plates identify wholesale dealers with **WX** and retail dealers **X**.
Apportioned vehicle plates begin with the numeric 9, and do not indicate the county of origin or the weight class.

**Kentucky Department of Vehicle Regulation, Motor Vehicle Licensing
Room 308, State Office Building, Frankfort, KY 40622   Tel. 502-564-5301**

LOUISIANA

POLICE PATCH

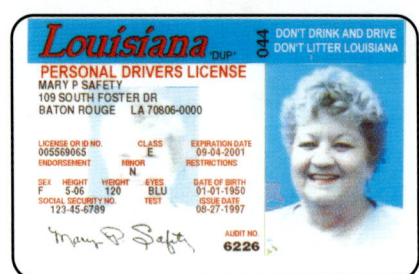

DRIVERS LICENSE

PASSENGER PLATES

PASSENGER
1 PLATE 1
DECAL

PERSONALIZED

HANDICAPPED
DEALER

DISABLED
VETERAN

HEARING
IMPAIRED

CIVIL AIR
PATROL

PEARL HARBOR
SURVIVOR

EDUCATOR

WILDLIFE

WILDLIFE

WILDLIFE

VOLUNTEER
FIREMAN

TRUCK AND TRAILER PLATES

APPORTIONED

TRUCK

PRIVATE

FARM TRUCK

PLATE VALIDATION

MO/YR

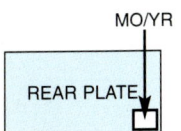

REAR PLATE

www.dps.la.us/omv.html

The "Sportsman's Paradise" issues one 3 alpha - 3 numeric fully-reflectorized passenger license plate. Recently all previously issued plates have been replaced with a new design featuring the state name in a "lipstick" script.

Distinctive captions:

ANTIQUE -Vehicle over 25 yrs.
CUT - City use Truck
FP- Forest products truck
FU - Farm Use
PO - Private owner
POS - Private semitrailer

PUBLIC - State, parish & municipal vehicles
SHRINER - Parade vehicle
STREET ROD - Modified vehicle made in USA before 1949
XPOW - Former prisoner of war
DV - Disabled veteran
GROTTO - Parade vehicle

Codes:

New passenger plates are 3 alpha - 3 numeric. Earlier issued passenger plates contain a single letter decal which designates the Louisiana State Police troop area in which the plate was issued:.

A	Baton Rouge	H	Leesville
B	New Orleans	I	Lafayette
C	Raceland	K	Opelousas
D	Lake Charles	L	Covington
E	Alexandria	N	New Orleans
F	Monroe	X	Baton Rouge &
G	Shreveport		statewide mail-out

Truck, trailer, commercial and other special vehicles are issued plates with an alpha prefix that indicates the vehicle class or special use.

A - Private bus,school bus, road tractor house trailer, commercial
B - Private truck 6,001- 18,000 lbs.
C - Common carrier truck,tractor
D - Light, boat and semi-trailer
E - Trailer
F - Farm vehicle

H - Handicapped person
J - Vehicle transporting forest products
M - City use
P- Apportioned
R, S,T - Private truck up to 6,000 lbs.
Y - Long-term trailer

Louisiana Department of Public Safety, Vehicle Registration Bureau
P.O. Box 64886, Baton Rouge, LA 70896   Tel. 504-925-6335

MAINE

POLICE PATCH

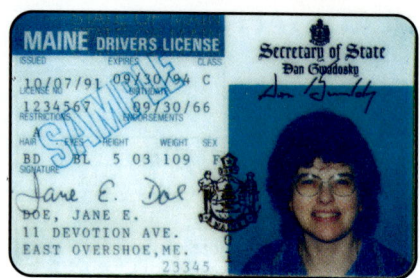

DRIVERS LICENSE

PASSENGER PLATES

PASSENGER

**PERSONALIZED
OLDER ISSUE**

ENVIRONMENT

**PENOBSCOT
NATION REP**

**COMBINATION
PRIVATE/COMM**

**DISABLED
VETERAN**

**MAINE HOUSE
OF REP.**

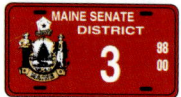

SENATE

CMH

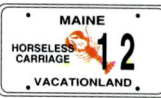

COLLECTOR

MUNICIPAL

**PERSONALIZED
NEW BASE**

TRUCK AND TRAILER PLATES

APPORTIONED

TRAILER

**APPORTIONED
TRAILER**

TRUCK

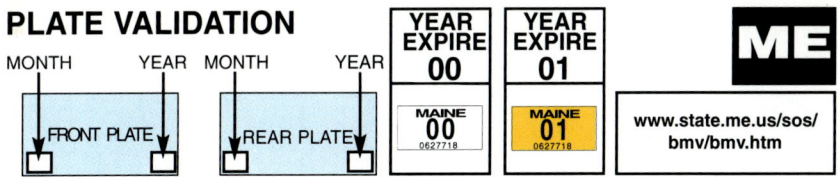

PLATE VALIDATION

MONTH   YEAR   MONTH   YEAR

FRONT PLATE   REAR PLATE

YEAR EXPIRE 00

MAINE 00 0627718

YEAR EXPIRE 01

MAINE 01 0627718

ME

www.state.me.us/sos/bmv/bmv.htm

America's "Vacationland" issues two fully-reflectorized plates; most have a red lobster graphic background. Until recently Maine passenger plates were all numeric. Currently they are being issued with a one or two letter suffix.

Distinctive captions:

COACH - Ambulance, funeral coach and hearse

INDIAN REPRESENTATIVE - Representative of Indian Tribes at the Maine State Legislature

EQUIPMENT- Towed equipment such as a cement mixer, etc.

LIVESTOCK AND POULTRY - Issued by Maine Dept. of Agriculture to livestock and poultry dealers

LT TRAILER - Long-term trailer registration

Codes:

Passenger vehicle plates have 1 - 6 characters (all numeric or 1 or 2 alpha suffix). All passenger plates are graphic, with the red lobster in the background. Commercial vehicle plates are all numeric and are clearly captioned.

The following prefix codes are used:

C		H -	Passenger veh. for hire
O	- All trucks and tractors	L -	Loaner
M		NC, UC -	New and Used car dlr.
C over R -	Conserve Resources	N G (suffix) -	National Guard
D -	Dealers	T -	Transporter
F -	Farm truck	V -	Veteran
F over F	Firefighter	W -	Wrecker

Maine does not issue special occupational plates or designate the county of origin, weight or use restriction on license plates.

Maine license plate numbering system
1-999999
1A-99999A
1B-99999Z
1AA-9999AA
1BB-9999ZZ
1AB-9999AB
AC,AD,etc;BA,BC,BD etc

Maine Secretary of State's Office, Bureau of Motor Vehicles
29 State House Station, Augusta, ME 04333   Tel. 207-287-8637

MARYLAND

POLICE PATCH

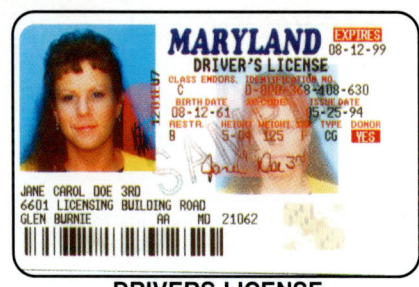

DRIVERS LICENSE

PASSENGER PLATES

PASSENGER
2 PLATES 2
DECALS ON
REAR

PERSONALIZED

HANDICAPPED

DISABLED
VETERAN

ENVIRONMENT

LOCAL
GOVERNMENT

STATE
GOVERNMENT

HAM RADIO

DEALER

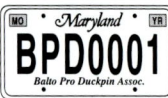

BOWLING
ASSOCIATION

FIREMAN'S
ASSOCIATION

NATIONAL
GUARD

TRUCK AND TRAILER PLATES

APPORTIONED

TRUCK OR
TRAILER

PLATE VALIDATION

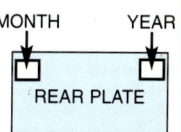

MONTH   YEAR

FRONT PLATE   REAR PLATE

YEAR EXPIRE **00**

YEAR EXPIRE **01**

www.mdot.state.md.us

The "Old Line State" issues two fully-reflectorized license plates. Passenger and many other non-passenger types display the colorful state shield. A special plate to save the Chesapeake Bay is available for an additional $20 fee.

Distinctive captions:

FARM AREA - Vehicles permitted to operate on public road adjacent to a farm
FINANCE - Repossessed vehicle transporter plate
RECYCLER - Auto wreckers and scrap processors
TRANS - Transporter

Codes:

Maryland passenger cars are issued 3 alpha-3 numeric plates. The following alpha combinations are reserved for specific classes of vehicles:

Suffix **B** - Taxi, limousine
Suffix **C** - Ambulance, funeral vehicle
DV - Disabled veteran
D over **R** -Daily rental
Suffix **D** - Dump service
Suffix **F** - Truck tractors
F over **T** - Farm truck
H over **C** - Handicapped
I (capital i) - Buses for hire

Suffix **J** - Passenger vans (van pool)
L over **G** - Local government
Suffix **K** - Farm vehicle limited highway use
Suffix **L** - Historic Motor vehicle
Suffix **M** - Multi-purpose trucks, vans
Suffix **PSC** - Buses for hire
S over **G** - State government vehicle
TT - Tow truck

Maryland reserves the following prefixes for special groups: * **no caption appears at the bottom of these plates.**

AG	Ali Ghan Shrine Temple	**FPO**	Frat. Order of Police	**OPT**	Optimist Club
AL	American Legion	**FMA**	Prince Hall Gr.Lodge	**OSI**	Sons of Italy
BBO*	Boumi Temple	**FSU**	Frostburg U. alumni	**PE**	Professional engineers
BCF	Balt.County firefighters	**GOP**	Republican Party	**PSU**	Penn State Alumni
BJT	Jerusalem Temple No 4	**HC**	Hood College	**PSY**	Psychological Assn
BNA*	B'nai B'rith	**HGA**	Hiram Grand Lodge	**PW**	Ex POW
BPD	Balt. Pro Duckpin Assn.	**HIQ**	Mensa	**QUE**	Omega Psi Phi Frat.
BPW	Md. Prof. bus. women	**HNA**	Holy Name Society	**RI**	Rotary International
BSA	Boy Scouts of America	**HPC**	Hawks Pleasure Club	**ROA**	Reserve Officers Assn.
BSQ	Barbershop Quartet sing.	**JC**	Jaycees	**RSC**	Ranger Social Club
CAP	Civil Air Patrol	**JHU**	Johns Hopkins Alumni	**RX**	Pharmacist Assn
CCC*	Grace Bible Church	**JWV**	Jewish War Veterans	**SKI**	Baltimore Ski Club
CDA	Cath. Dau. of America	**KAP**	Kappa Alpha Psi	**SMC**	St Marys College alum.
CGA	Coast Guard Auxiliary	**KC**	Knights of Columbus	**TCL**	Tall Cedars
CGR	Coast Guard Reserve	**KOP**	Knights of Pythias	**TJA**	Trial Judges Assn
CMH	Medal of Honor	**LHS**	Loyola H.S. alumni	**TPA**	Telephone Pioneers
DAV	Disabled Amer.veteran	**LCO**	Lions Club International	**TSU**	Towson State Alumni
DCC	St. Dem. Cntrl Comm.	**M** over**D**	Maryland Democratic party	**UAW**	Unit. Auto Workers 239
DDS	Dr. of Dental Surgery			**UM**	Univ. of Maryland Alum.
EAA	Exper. Aircraft Assn.	**MP**	Maryland Press Club	**VFW**	Vet. of Foreign Wars
EEE	Free State Square Club	**MSA**	Maryland Soc. Account.	**VPI**	Virginia Tech
ELK	Elks Club	**MSP**	Md. St. Police Assn.	**WMC**	West Virginia Univ.
FOE	Frat. Order of Eagles	Suffix **NG**	National Guard	**WVU**	West Va. Univ.
FF	MD, DC Firefighters	**ND**	Notre Dame Club	**VB**	Vulcan Blazers
				YG*	Yedz Grotto

Maryland does not designate the county or weight of a vehicle on the plate.

Maryland Motor Vehicle Administration
6601 Ritchie Highway NE, Glen Burnie, MD 21062   Tel. 410-787-2983

MASSACHUSETTS

POLICE PATCH

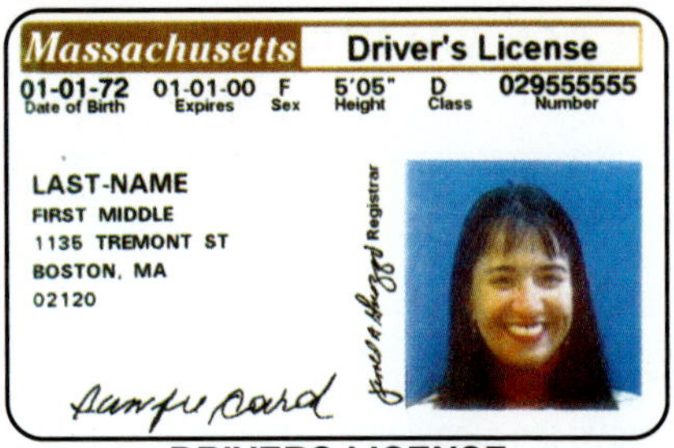

DRIVERS LICENSE

PASSENGER PLATES

Massachusetts MO/YR
123-ZBC
The Spirit of America

PASSENGER

Massachusetts NOV/YR
PILGRM
The Spirit of America

PERSONALIZED

MASSACHUSETTS MO/YR
123·456

PASSENGER OLDER BASE

APR **Massachusetts** YR
1234
The Spirit of America

RESERVED SERIES

Massachusetts
R/W 12AB
Preserve the Trust

ENVIRONMENT SAVE THE WHALE

·**Massachusetts**·
C/I 12AB
Cape Cod & Islands

ENVIRONMENT CAPE COD

Massachusetts NOV/YR
AA11
Veteran

VETERAN

S E N A T E **Massachusetts**
12
The Spirit of America

SENATE

·**Massachusetts**·
22345
· Pupils ·

PRIVATE SCHOOL BUS

Massachusetts MO/YR
K1·DRN
The Spirit of America

HAM RADIO

DCT **Massachusetts**
W1234
Preserve the Trust

TROUT PLATE

DCT **Massachusetts**
V0000
Preserve the Trust

INDUSTRIAL HERITAGE

TRUCK AND TRAILER PLATES

· **Massachusetts** · YR
47042
· APPORTIONED ·

APPORTIONED

· **Massachusetts** · MO/YR
103-193
· COMMERCIAL ·

COMMERCIAL

· **Massachusetts** · YR
123-456
· SEMI-TRAILER ·

SEMI-TRAILER

PLATE VALIDATION

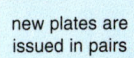
new plates are issued in pairs

MO/YR
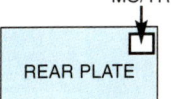
REAR PLATE

YEAR EXPIRE 00
Massachusetts 2000 B. 667450

YEAR EXPIRE 01
Massachusetts 2001 B. 667450

www.state.ma.us.rev

MA

The "Bay State" issues two fully-reflectorized graphic license plates. Earlier-issued green on white plates are still in use. Many plates are being manufactured on the newer red, white and blue "The Spirit of America" base .

Distinctive captions:

ANTIQUE- A vehicle at least 25 years old
BOATS- Boat and boat trailer dealer
REPAIR- Towing of motor vehicles & trailers
CAMPER- Autohome
HOUSE- Massachusetts House of Representatives member
NEWS PHOTOG - News photographer
PUPILS- Private carrier vehicles for school children

Codes:

Passenger plates are 4 numeric- 2 alpha, 3 numeric- 3 alpha, 3 alpha-3 numeric, and all numeric.. Some low number plates have the month of expiration embossed. Truck and trailer plates can be all numeric and captioned COMMERCIAL or TRAILER . Some older truck and trailer plates have an alpha prefix A,B,C and some have two alphas stacked as a prefix.
  Massachusetts does not use county or weight codes on plates.

The last numeric on a regular passenger plate is an expiration code:

1 - January	5 - May	9 - September
2- February	6 - June	0 - October
3 - March	7 - July	
4 - April	8- August	

The following alpha prefixes are reserved for special use:

AMB Ambulance
BRUINS Member and team number
CELTICS Member and team number
DLR Dealer
DLR RV Recreational vehicle dealer
EX POW Former prisoner of war
MD Medical doctor
MDC Metropolitan District Commission
NG National Guard

Massachusetts Registry of Motor Vehicles
1135 Tremont St., Boston, MA 02110   Tel. 617-351-2700

MICHIGAN

POLICE PATCH

DRIVERS LICENSE

PASSENGER PLATES

PASSENGER
1 PLATE 2
DECALS

PERSONALIZED

HANDICAPPED

OPTIONAL
GRAPHIC

AUTO 100 YRS

SHERIFF

FIREMAN

VETERAN
WW111

PURPLE HEART

LIONS CLUB

PLATE NAME

PLATE NAME

TRUCK AND TRAILER PLATES

TRUCK GVW

APPORTIONED
TRUCK

5 YR TRAILER

APPORTIONED
TRAILER

PLATE VALIDATION

MONTH   YEAR

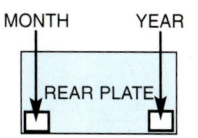

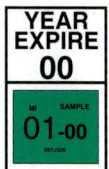

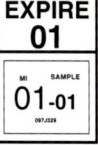

www.sos.state.mi.us

The "Great Lakes State" issues one partially-reflectorized (glass beads on paint background) white on blue license plate. Personalized plates are issued in pairs . Special graphic plates recognizing the Mackinac Bridge and the 100th anniversary of the automobile are available as optional issues for an additional fee.

Distinctive captions:

IN TRANSIT REPAIR - Non-dealer auto transport and service
SPECIAL EQUIPMENT - Construction equipment
MANUFACTURER - New untitled vehicles operated by manufacturers
REPOSSESSION- Used by financial institutions to repossess cars
SPECIAL FARM -Transporter of farm crops from field to storage
SCHOOL BUS - Non-profit organization school bus, and van vehicle

Codes:

Michigan passenger plates are 3 alpha - 3 numeric and reverse.
special graphic optional plates are 3 alpha -2 numeric
The following prefixes are reserved for special use:

DV	Disabled veteran	**25Y-29Y**	Non-profit organization
MSG	State owned vehicle	**90Y**	Civil Air Patrol
REP	State Representative	**DNR**	Dept. of Natural Resources
SEN	State Senator		

All numeric characters on a plate indicates a state or government-owned vehicle.
The first 2 numerics on state-owned plates indicate the following:
01	Mich. Dept. of Transportation automobile
02	Mich. Dept. of Transportation pickup truck
03 - 05	Mich. Dept. of Transportation heavy equipment
08, 09	Passenger vehicle state transportation pool- use by all depts
11	Passenger vehicle assigned to an individual state agency
12, 13,16	Vehicles assigned to Dept. of Natural Resources
71, 72	State-owned vans used as small buses

Other special prefixes:

3 numeric - **D** Auto dealer
2 numeric - **M** Manufacturer
2 numeric - **T** Transporter
2 numeric - **R** Repossessor
2 numeric - **X** Municipal

2 numeric - **Y** Non-profit organization
2 numeric - **CE** Civic event vehicle
2 numeric - **F** Special farm vehicle
2 numeric - **G** In-transit repair

Trucks for hire, buses and taxis have 4 numeric - 2 alpha plates.
The weight class of trucks over 24,000 lbs. GVW appears on a
sticker placed at the bottom of the plate.
Trailer plates for 1-year use are: 1 alpha-5 numerics -1 alpha.
Trailer plates for 5-year use are: 1 alpha(A or B) - 5 numerics -1(A or B).

MINNESOTA

POLICE PATCH

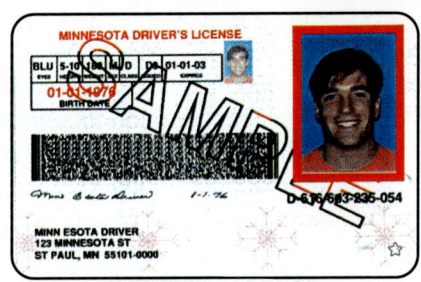

DRIVERS LICENSE

PASSENGER PLATES

PASSENGER
2 PLATES 2
DECALS

OLDER ISSUE

PERSONALIZED

STATE OWNED

HANDICAPPED

CRITICAL
HABITAT

DEALER

TAX EXEMPT

COLLEGIATE
(14 SCHOOLS
AVAILABLE)

VET LAOS

PURPLE HEART

RESTRICTED
USE PLATE

TRUCK AND TRAILER PLATES

APPORTIONED
TRUCK

TRUCK
COMMERCIAL
ZONE

TRUCK
COMMERCIAL

FARM TRUCK

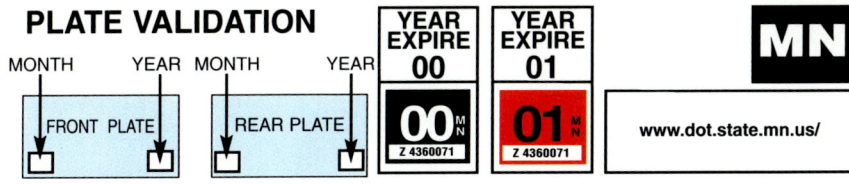

PLATE VALIDATION

MONTH   YEAR MONTH   YEAR

FRONT PLATE   REAR PLATE

YEAR EXPIRE **00**

YEAR EXPIRE **01**

00 M N   Z 4360071

01 M N   Z 4360071

MN

www.dot.state.mn.us/

The "Land of 10,000 Lakes" issues two fully-reflectorized license plates. Most non-passenger vehicle plates are non-graphic.

Distinctive captions:

CLASSIC CAR - Restored vehicles manufactured between 1925 and 1948
COLLECTOR - Restored vehicle manufactured after 1935 at least 25 years old
PIONEER - Restored vehicle manufactured prior to 1936
TAX EXEMPT - Vehicle owned by state or political subdivision

Codes:

Passenger plates are 3 numeric - 3 alpha. There are no county codes.
Truck and truck tractor plates are numeric and use alpha prefixes:
F over **T** - farm trailer
Y over **A** -or any combination of Y and another alpha- general purpose truck
Y over **T**- General purpose trailer
T over **L** or **M** - Farm truck with restricted highway use
T over **T** - Farm tractor
P over **R** with **L** prefix - Prorated tractor units. The L can be other alphas
P over **T** with **R** prefix- Prorated trailers. R can be other alphas
C over **Z** - Trucks restricted to operation in the commercial zone of cities
LM prefix - Commercial limousine

Trucks and trailer plates display weight class decals:

Decal code	Gross wgt. in lbs.	Decal code	Gross wgt. in lbs.
E	up to 9,000	N	45,001 - 51,000
F	9001 - 12000	O	51,001 - 57,000
G	12,001- 15,000	P	57,001 - 63,000
H	15,001-18,000	Q	63,001 - 69,000
I	18,001-21,000	R	69,001 - 73,270
J	21,001- 27,000	S+6S	73,271 - 77,000
K	27,001 - 33,000	T+6T	77,001 - 81,000
L	33,001- 39,000	X+6X	Special permit over 81,000 lbs
M	39,001 - 45,000	6	indicates vehicle must use 6 axles

other codes:
B over **Y** prefix- Charter bus
BDU - Duluth transit bus
D - Dealer
IC - Intercity bus
K - Citizens band radio call sign
R - Recreational vehicle

S over **B** - Contract school bus
WX,WY,XW- Special plate issued by a court when the owner has been convicted and the plates impounded. These plates permit law enforcement to stop and inspect the vehicle and driver at any time (often used in cases of DUI).

Minnesota Department of Public Safety, Driver and Vehicle Services Div.
123 Transportation Bldg., 395 John Ireland Blvd., St Paul, MN 55155   Tel. 612-296-2001

MISSISSIPPI

POLICE PATCH

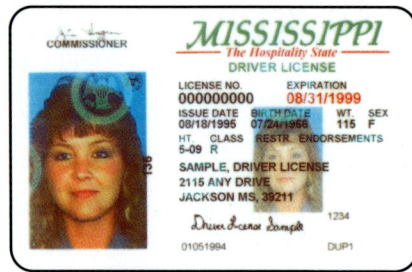

DRIVERS LICENSE

PASSENGER PLATES

PASSENGER
1 PLATE 2
DECALS

PERSONALIZED

COLLEGIATE

WILDLIFE

WILDLIFE

VETERAN
BRANCH
OPTIONAL

HIGHWAY
PATROL

LAW
ENFORCEMENT

COLLEGIATE
OLE MISS

COLLEGIATE
JACKSON
STATE UNIV.

COLLEGIATE
STATE
UNIVERSITY

OLDER BASE

TRUCK AND TRAILER PLATES

APPORTIONED

TRUCK

SEMI-TRAILER

FARM

PLATE VALIDATION

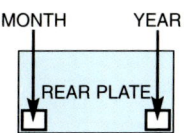

MONTH   YEAR

REAR PLATE

YEAR EXPIRE 00	YEAR EXPIRE 01

www.state.ms.us/

"The Magnolia State issues one fully-reflectorized license plate. The county name is embossed on all passenger and light truck plates.

Distinctive captions:

ANTIQUE CAR - A vehicle 25 years or older
100% DAV - Veteran totally disabled - service connected
NC BUS - Non-commercial bus
TAX FREE- Municipal government vehicle
TEMPORARY FARM - 3 - 6 month vehicle registration

Codes:

Private passenger car plates have 3 alpha - 3 numeric characters and the county of origin appears on the bottom of the plate. The alpha numeric combinations are for individual vehicle identification only and have no hidden codes.

State officials and state-owned vehicles have the following codes:

1 - Governor
2 - Lt. Governor
X1, X2 - Former Gov, & Lt. Gov.

SO - Sheriff's office.
(**1** is Sheriff, **2** and up deputies)
X US CONGRESS - Former congressman
X US SENATE - Former senator

Trucks, truck tractors, trailers and other commercial vehicles have an alpha numeric prefix on the left side of the plate. The alpha indicates the use and the numeric the weight class in thousands of pounds.

B - Truck for hire
CC - Common carrier bus
F - Farm vehicle(hauling own property)
G - Tax-exempt government agency
H - **BUS** - Vehicle for hire (max 7 pass.)

H - DRAY - Truck for hire (5 mile area).
HH - Moving van for hire.
NC - BUS - Non-commercial bus
TLR - Trailer

The following numerics appear immediately after the alpha prefix and indicate the gross vehicle weight in thousands of pounds:

10	26	40	46	52	58	64	72	78
16	30	42	48	54	60	66	74	80-
20	36	44	50	56	62	68	76	max

Mississippi State Tax Commission, Motor Vehicle Licensing
P.O.Box 1033, Jackson , MS 39215   Tel. 601-359-1248

MISSOURI

POLICE PATCH

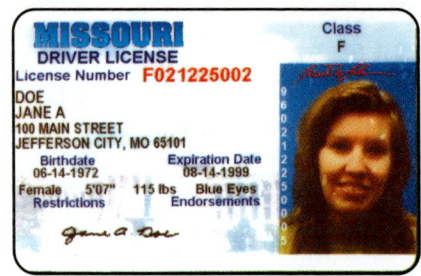

DRIVERS LICENSE

PASSENGER PLATES

PASSENGER
2 PLATES, 2
DECALS ON BOTH

PERSONALIZED

HANDICAPPED

**NATIONAL
GUARD**

FORMER POW

**HIGHWAY
PATROL**

NAVY RESERVE

CMH

**COLLEGIATE
ST LOUIS UNIV.**

**COLLEGIATE
COLLEGE OF
OZARK**

**COLLEGIATE
MISS. STATE
UNIV.**

FIREMAN

TRUCK AND TRAILER PLATES

APPORTIONED

**TRAILER
PERMANENT**

**TRUCK
BEYOND
LOCAL**

**TRUCK LOCAL
6M**

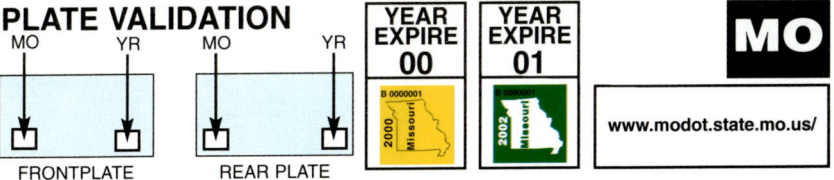

PLATE VALIDATION

FRONTPLATE	REAR PLATE
MO YR	MO YR

YEAR EXPIRE 00

YEAR EXPIRE 01

MO

www.modot.state.mo.us/

The "Show-Me State" issues two partially-reflectorized license plates (glass beads on paint background). On passenger plates the expiration decal appears in the middle of the rear plate. Collegiate plates are fully reflectorized. A new graphic general issue is being phased-in during 1997.

Distinctive captions:

SHOW-ME STATE- State nickname
DRIVE AWAY - Transporter plate (other than dealer)
HISTORIC VEHICLE - Restored vehicle over 25 years old
OFFICIAL CAR - State-owned vehicle

Codes:

Passenger license plates have 3 alpha - 3 numeric characters, also A1B-234 format.
The first alpha indicates the month of expiration:

A, V - JAN	**G, H** - MAY	**Q, Z** - DEC
B, D - FEB	**J, K** - JUN	**S, W** - SEP
C, L - MAR	**M, N** - JUL	**X, T** - OCT
E, F - APR	**P, R** - AUG	PERSONALIZED - JUL

Other codes:

D - Dealer
DV - Disabled Veteran
R - State Representative

S - State Senator
HP - State Highway Patrol
USS, USC - US Senate, Congress

Missouri does not indicate county of origin on license plates.

Truck plates are issued to all motor vehicles used for transportation of property. Fees are based on gross weight (combined weight of the vehicle and the load) and zone of operation either local or beyond-local.

Truck, trailer and bus codes that appear on the top or bottom of the plate:

L - (Local)Limited to a municipality and 25 miles beyond
BL - Can operate beyond local area
Apportioned - Interstate operator

L BUS - Local bus, 25 mile area
T BUS - Transit bus
C BUS - Commercial bus

The small numeric that appears in conjunction with the above codes indicates the weight class for trucks, and the number of passengers for transit and commercial buses.

Trucks in the 12,000 lb-and-under class are issued plates with an alpha expiration code the same as passenger plates. Heavier truck and bus plates are all numeric:

100,001 - 500,000 local;   500,001 - 800,000 beyond local

Missouri Department of Revenue, Division of Motor Vehicles
Harry S. Truman State Office Building
P.O.Box 100, Jefferson City MO 65105   Tel. 573-751- 4429

61

MONTANA

POLICE PATCH

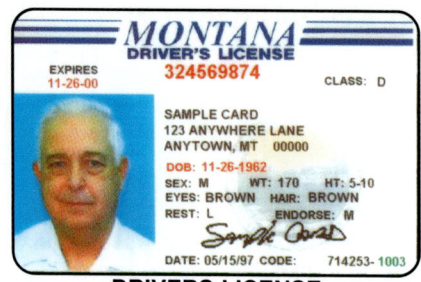

DRIVERS LICENSE

PASSENGER PLATES

**PASSENGER
NEW YR. 2000**

OLDER BASE

PERSONALIZED

DISABLED

STATE OWNED

**MARINE
VETERAN**

**NATIONAL
GUARD**

COLLECTOR

**COLLEGIATE
NMC**

**COLLEGIATE
UNIV. OF
MONTANA**

HAM RADIO

TRUCK AND TRAILER PLATES

APPORTIONED

TRUCK

TRAILER

PLATE VALIDATION

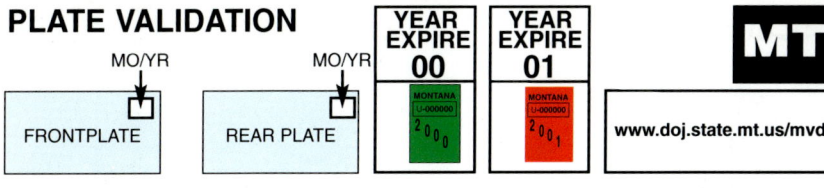

| MO/YR | MO/YR | YEAR EXPIRE 00 | YEAR EXPIRE 01 |

FRONTPLATE   REAR PLATE

www.doj.state.mt.us/mvd

MT

"Big Sky Country" issues two fully-reflectorized license plates. The numeric prefix indicates the county of origin.

Distinctive captions:

EXEMPT - County-owned vehicle
PIONEER - Vehicle manufactured in 1933 or earlier.
VINTAGE - Vehicle more than 30 years old, manufactured in 1934 or later.

Codes:

The first 1 or 2 numeric characters on passenger, truck and large trailer plates is a county code; passenger plates under 10 have an alpha P. The county code (county seats) are :

1P - Silver Bow (Butte)
2P - Cascade (Great Falls)
3P - Yellowstone (Billings)
4P - Missoula (Missoula)
5P - Lewis & Clark (Helena)
6P - Gallatin (Bozeman)
7P - Flathead (Kalispell)
8P - Fergus (Lewistown)
9P - Powder River (Broadus)
10 - Carbon (Red Lodge)
11 - Phillips - (Malta)
12 - Hill (Havre)
13 - Ravalli (Hamilton)
14 - Custer (Miles City)
15 - Lake (Polson)
16 - Dawson (Glendive)
17 - Roosevelt (Wolf Point)
18 - Beaverhead (Dillon)
19 - Chouteau (Ft. Benton)
20 - Valley (Glasgow)

21 - Toole (Shelby)
22 - Big Horn (Hardin)
23 - Musselshell (Roundup)
24 - Blaine (Chinook)
25 - Madison (Virginia City)
26 - Pondera (Conrad)
27 - Richland (Sidney)
28 - Powell (Deer Lodge)
29 - Rosebud (Forsyth)
30 - Deer Lodge (Anaconda)
31 - Teton (Chouteau)
32 - Stillwater (Columbus)
33 - Treasure (Hysham)
34 - Sheridan (Plentywood)
35 - Sanders (ThompsonFalls)
36 - Judith Basin (Stanford)
37 - Daniels (Scobey)
38 - Glacier (Cut Bank)
39 - Fallon -(Baker)

40 - Sweet Grass (Big Timber)
41 - McCone (Circle)
42 - Carter (Ekalaka)
43 - Broadwater (Townsend)
44 - Wheatland (Harlowton)
45 - Prairie (Terry)
46 - Granite (Philipsburg)
47 - Meagher (Whte Sul Spgs)
48 - Liberty (Chester)
49 - Park (Livingston)
50 - Garfield (Jordan)
51 - Jefferson (Boulder)
52 - Wibaux (Wibaux)
53 - Golden Valley (Ryegate)
54 - Mineral (Superior)
55 - Petroleum (Winnett)
56 - Lincoln (Libby)

Alpha characters indicate the following:

CC- Carroll College
CGF- College of Great Falls
D -Dealer
DCC- Dawson Community Col.
DS-Driver service
EMC- Eastern Mt. Col.
FG-Fish & Game Comm.
FVC- Flathead Valley Community College

H-State Highway Dept.
M- State-owned vehicle
MCC- Miles Comm. Col.
MHP- Mt. Highway Patrol
MSP- Mt State Prison
MSU- Mt. State Univ.
MT- Montana Tech.
NMC- Northern Mt. Col.
RMC - Rocky Mtn. Col.

P- (prefix)Truck tractor (Power)
SKC- Salish Kootenai Col.
T-Truck
T over R - Trailer
UD- Used car dealer
UM- Univ. of Montana
WMC- Western Montana College

Montana does not designate the weight of a vehicle on the license plate.

Montana Department of Justice, Registrar of Motor Vehicles
1032 Buckskin Drive, Deer Lodge, MT 59722   Tel. 406-846-6000

NEBRASKA

POLICE PATCH

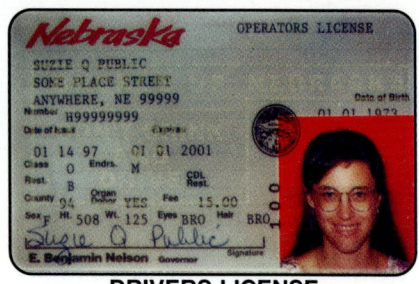

DRIVERS LICENSE

PASSENGER PLATES

PASSENGER
2 PLATES 1
DECAL ON
BOTH

PASSENGER
OLDER BASE

PERSONALIZED

HANDICAPPED

PURPLE HEART

STATE OWNED

COUNTY
OWNED

DEALER

AMATEUR
RADIO

COLLEGIATE
UNIV. OF NE

TRUCK AND TRAILER PLATES

APP **PERMANENT** PWR **P 12345** **NEBRASKA**	TON **NEBR** **TRUCK** MO-YR 94 LOCL 1234	**APPORTIONED** **P 12345** **NEB POWER**	**APPORTIONED** PERM 78310 **NEB TRAILER**
APPORTIONED	TRUCK LOCAL USE	APPORTIONED POWER UNIT	TRAILER APP. PERMANENT

PLATE VALIDATION

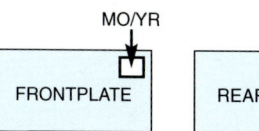

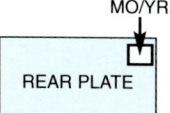

The "Cornhusker State" issues two fully-reflectorized license plates. The numeric prefix indicates the county of origin. Nebraska generally replaces all plates every 3 years with the exception of: Government, Tax Exempt and Historical plates which are considered permanent.

Distinctive captions:

APP - Apportioned
COMM - Commercial vehicles for hire and equipped to carry cargo
LOCL - Commercial vehicle limited to 10 mile area of operations
HISTORICAL - A restored vehicle 30 years old or older

R - Repossession plate used by finance companies
T - Transporter of vehicles not their own, for delivery
BX -Boat dealer
FV - Movie or TV production vehicle

Codes:

Nebraska passenger vehicle license plates have a numeric county prefix followed by an alpha and numerics. Truck plates have the same county prefix followed by captions: **COMM**, **LOCAL**, **FARM** and **AGR**.

The county prefixes and (county seats) are as follows:

1 - Douglas (Omaha)
2 - Lancaster (Lincoln)
3 - Gage (Beatrice)
4 - Custer (Broken Bow)
5 - Dodge (Fremont)
6 - Saunders (Wahoo)
7 - Madison (Madison)
8 - Hall (Grand Island)
9 - Buffalo (Kearney)
10 - Platte (Columbus)
11 - Otoe (Nebraska City)
12 - Knox (Center)
13 - Cedar (Hartington)
14 - Adams (Hastings)
15 - Lincoln (North Platte)
16 - Seward (Seward)
17 - York (York)
18 - Dawson (Lexington)
19 - Richardson (Falls Cty)
20 - Cass (Plattsmouth)
21 - Scotts Bluff (Gering)
22 - Saline (Wilber)
23 - Boone (Albion)
24 - Cuming (West Point)
25 - Butler (David City)
26 - Antelope (Neligh)
27 - Wayne (Wayne)
28 - Hamilton (Aurora)
29 - Washington (Blair)
30 - Clay (Clay Center)
31 - Burt (Tekamah)

32 - Thayer (Hebron)
33 - Jefferson (Fairbury)
34 - Fillmore (Geneva)
35 - Dixon (Ponca)
36 - Holt (O'Neill)
37 - Phelps (Holdrege)
38 - Furnas (Beaver City)
39 - Cheyenne (Sidney)
40 - Pierce (Pierce)
41 - Polk (Osceola)
42 - Nuckolls (Nelson)
43 - Colfax (Schuyler)
44 - Nemaha (Auburn)
45 - Webster (Red Cloud)
46 - Merrick (Central City)
47 - Valley (Ord)
48 - Red Willow (McCook)
49 - Howard (St. Paul)
50 - Franklin (Franklin)
51 - Harlan (Alma)
52 - Kearney (Minden)
53 - Stanton (Stanton)
54 - Pawnee (Pawnee City)
55 - Thurston (Pender)
56 - Sherman (Loup City)
57 - Johnson (Tecumseh)
58 - Nance (Fullerton)
59 - Sarpy (Papillion)
60 - Frontier (Stockville)
61 - Sheridan (Rushville)
62 - Greeley (Greeley)

63 - Boyd (Butte)
64 - Morrill (Bridgeport)
65 - Box Butte (Alliance)
66 - Cherry (Valentine)
67 - Hitchcock (Trenton)
68 - Keith (Ogallala)
69 - Dawes ((Chadron)
70 - Dakota (Dakota City)
71 - Kimball (Kimball)
72 - Chase (Imperial)
73 - Gosper (Elwood)
74 - Perkins (Grant)
75 - Brown (Ainsworth)
76 - Dundy (Benkelman)
77 - Garden (Oshkosh)
78 - Deuel (Chappell)
79 - Hayes (Hayes Center)
80 - Sioux (Harrison)
81 - Rock - (Bassett)
82 - Keya Paha (Springview)
83 - Garfield (Burwell)
84 - Wheeler (Bartlett)
85 - Banner (Harrisburg)
86 - Blaine (Brewster)
87 - Logan (Stapleton)
88 - Loup (Taylor)
89 - Thomas (Thedford)
90 - McPherson (Tryon)
91 - Arthur (Arthur)
92 - Grant (Hyannis)
93 - Hooker (Mullen)

All Nebraska registered trucks carry a tonnage sticker on their license plate.

Nebraska Department of Motor Vehicles, Registration and Titles Division
301 Centennial Mall South, P.O.Box 94789, Lincoln NE 68509-4789   Tel. 402-471-3918

NEVADA

POLICE PATCH

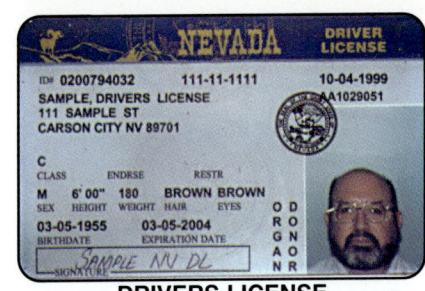

DRIVERS LICENSE

PASSENGER PLATES

PASSENGER

PERSONALIZED

PASSENGER
OLDER BASE
1996

PASSENGER
OLDER BASE

CENTENNIAL

PASSSENGER
OLDER BASE

HANDICAPPED

VETERAN

LAKE TAHOE

DEALER

CITY/STATE
/COUNTY

PLATE NAME

TRUCK AND TRAILER PLATES

APPORTIONED
TRUCK

TRUCK

TRAILER
APPORTIONED

SEMI-TRAILER

PLATE VALIDATION

MO/YR

YEAR EXPIRE 00	YEAR EXPIRE 01

www.state.nv.us

FRONT PLATE   REAR PLATE

The "Silver State" issues two fully-reflective license plates. The last general re-issue of plates was in 1969. Since then five styles of plates have been issued and are still valid.

Distinctive captions:

E X - Tax-exempt (state / city / county) vehicle
DOT- Nevada Dept. of Transportation
OLD TIMER - Collector's vehicle 40 yrs. or older.
HORSELESS CARRIAGE - Collector's veh.1915 or older.
BODY SHOP- Test drive vehicle under repair
LOAN - Loaner plate used by body shop.

Codes:

The 1969 base passenger plates with an alpha county code prefix are still in use. These codes are:

C, CA - CZ, CAA - CZZ: Clark (Las Vegas)
CH, CHA - CHZ: Churchill (Fallon)
DAA - DZZ, DS, DSA - DSZ: Douglas (Minden)
EAA - EZZ, EL, ELA - ELZ: Elko (Elko)
ES, ESA - ESZ: Esmeralda (Goldfield)
EU - Eureka (Eureka)
FAA, FZZ - Churchill (Fallon)
HU, HUA - HUZ: Humboldt (Winnemucca)
KAA - KZZ: Washoe (Reno)
LA, LAA - LAZ- Lander (Austin)
LN, LNA - LNZ- Lincoln (Pioche)
LY, LYA - LYZ, LBA - LZZ: Lyon (Yerington)

MAA - MZZ, MN, MNA - MNZ: Mineral (Hawthorne)
NAA - NZZ, NA, NYA - NYZ: Nye (Tonopah)
OAA - OZZ, OR, ORA - ORZ: Ormsby (Carson City)
PAA - PZZ, PE, PEA - PEZ: Pershing (Lovelock)
ST, STA - STZ: Storey (Virginia City)
TAA -TZZ: Clark (Las Vegas)
W, WAA - WZZ: Washoe (Reno)
WP, WPA - WPZ: White Pine (Ely)
ZAA - ZZZ: White Pine (Ely)

Truck and truck tractor plates issued before 1982 have a county prefix code:

AA - AZ Churchill	**GA - GZ** Eureka	**MA - MZ** Mineral	**WA - WZ** Washoe
BA - BZ Clark	**HA - HZ** Humboldt	**OA - OZ** Carson City	**YA - YZ** Clark
DA - DZ Douglas	**JA - JZ** Lander	**NA - NZ** Nye	**ZA - ZZ** White Pine
EA - EZ Elko	**KA - KZ** Lincoln	**PA - PZ** Pershing	
FA - FZ Esmeralda	**LB - LZ** Lyon	**SA - SZ** Storey	

Trailer plates issued before 1982 have 1 alpha- 5 numeric characters. The current issue plate format is reversed. There are no county or weight codes.
The following suffixes and prefixes have special significance:
P - Prorated truck registration fee   **T** - Prorated trailer registration fee

Nevada requires all trucks over 5,000 lbs to display Motor Carrier Tax plate in addition to vehicle registration plates. The tax codes are:

Suffix **B** - 2 axle trucks under 10,000 lbs operating 50 miles either side CA/ NV border.
    C - Truck permitted to operate only within city limit and 5 miles beyond
    M - Indicates Weight Fee or Mileage tax method of payment.
    V - A convoy plate issued to transport vehicles.
    X - Indicates mileage tax method of payment
Nevada does not indicate the weight class of a truck, tractor or trailer by any code on the registration plate.

Nevada Department of Motor Vehicles & Public Safety
555 Wright Way, Carson City, NV 89711   Tel. 702- 687-3076

NEW HAMPSHIRE

POLICE PATCH

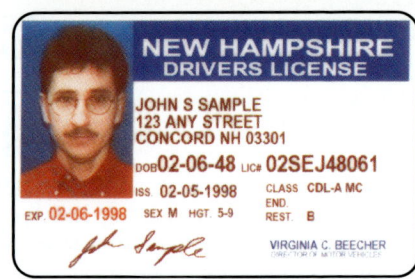

DRIVERS LICENSE

PASSENGER PLATES

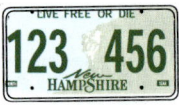

PASSENGER
2 PLATES 2
DECALS ON
BOTH

NEW ALT.
FORMAT

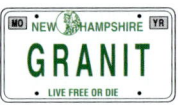

PERSONALIZED

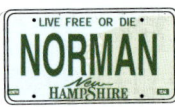

PERSONALIZED
ALT. FORMAT

ANTIQUE

DEALER

DISABLED
VETERAN

HANDICAPPED

STATE POLICE

NATIONAL
GUARD

TRUCK AND TRAILER PLATES

APPORTIONED

COMMERCIAL

FARM

TRAILER

PLATE VALIDATION

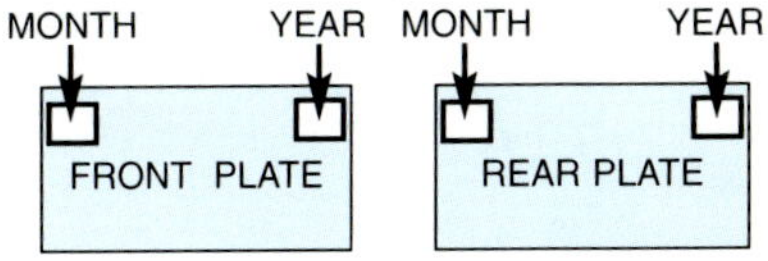

MONTH   YEAR   MONTH   YEAR

FRONT PLATE   REAR PLATE

YEAR EXPIRE **00**	YEAR EXPIRE **01**	
NEW HAMPSHIRE **2000** 048002100	NEW HAMPSHIRE **2001** 048002100	**NH** www.state.nh.us/dot

The "Granite State" issues two fully-reflectorized license plates with the unique slogan "Live Free or Die". Two different numbering systems are in use for passenger plates. Earlier issue plates are all numeric, while the current issue is three alpha - three numeric.

Distinctive captions:

JUDICIAL - Judge, Supreme Court, Superior Court
PERMANENT- County, city or town-owned vehicle
SHERIFF (1-10) - Sheriff of one of New Hampshire's 10 counties
SHERIFF DEPT - Deputies and staff
VETERAN - Disabled veteran

Codes:

Private passenger cars are issued green on white plates and there are no county codes.

Commercial and special class vehicle plates or alpha and numeric. They contain no county or weight codes, but the alpha character indicates as follows:

Prefix
A - All commercial plates begin with A
AMB - Ambulance
J - Junk dealer
R - Licensed repairman
SB - School bus
T - Transporter or trailer
T over **A** - Tractor
U - Utility dealer plate

Suffix
AG - Agricultural vehicle highway use limited to within 20 miles of farm
AN - Collector's veh.at least 25 yrs old
FA - Farm vehicle- unlim. highway use
T - Trailer

State government vehicle plates have an alpha prefix that is a department code:

A - Administration	**E** - Education	**NG** - National Guard
AE - Aeronautics	**ES** - Water Supply Control	**P** - Public health
AGR - Agriculture	**F** - Fish & Game	**S** - Safety
B - Banking	**M** - General code for	**SW** -Sweepstakes
C - Civil Defense	depts with few veh.	**T** - Tax
COR - Prison Industries	**H** - Highway	**TR** - Trailers
D - Recreation &	**L** - Liquor	**U** - University system
Economics	**LA** - Labor	**Y** - Industrial

New Hampshire Motor Vehicle Division
10 Hazen Drive, Concord, NH 03305   Tel. 603-271-2484

NEW JERSEY

POLICE PATCH

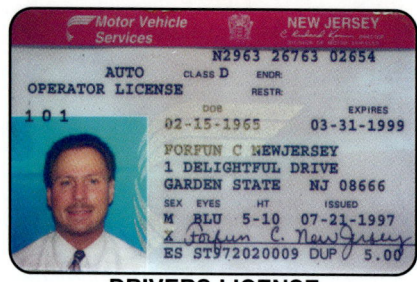

DRIVERS LICENSE

PASSENGER PLATES

PASSENGER
2 PLATES NEW
ISSUE DECAL

PASSENGER
OLDER BASE

COURTESY
PLATE

HANDICAPPED

SENATOR

CMH

ENVIRONMENT
EAGLE

CONSERVATION
SEASHORE

ENVIRONMENT
BAYMEN

ENVIRONMENT
PINELANDS

FRIENDS OF
ANIMALS

BATTLESHIP

TRUCK AND TRAILER PLATES

APPORTIONED

COMMERCIAL

COMMERCIAL

TRAILER

PLATE VALIDATION

YEAR EXPIRE **00**	YEAR EXPIRE **01**
20 New Jersey 00 **11**	New Jersey **11**

FRONT PLATE	REAR PLATE	www.state.nj.us/mvs

The "Garden State" has reflectorized plates. In 1999 they began using validation stickers on the plates replacing windshield stickers formerly used. Passenger cars will continue to be issued 2 plates.

Codes:

New Jersey issues 3 alpha - 3 numeric, 3 numeric -3 alpha, 2 alpha-3 numeric-1 alpha plates to passenger vehicles. Courtesy plates (reserved number series) have a maximum of 5 characters, usually 3 alpha either preceded or followed by 1 or 2 numerics.

Reserved prefixes

AB- Airborne	**ML- Marine Corp League Leathernecks**
AF- Air Force Reserve	**MM-** Merchant Marine
AL- American Legion	**MR-** Marine Reserve
AR- Army Reserve	**NG-** National Guard
AV- Amvets	**NR-** Naval Reserve
CA- Coast Guard Auxiliary	**NJP-** New Jersey Press
CI- Combat Infantryman Badge	**NYP-** New York Press
CMH- Congressional Medal of Honor	**P-** POW
CR - Coast Guard Reserve	**PB-** Police Benevolent Assn.
CW- Conserve Wildlife	**PA-** Telephone Pioneers
DD- Tin Can Sailors	**PS-** Penn State Alumni
DDS,DMD- Dentist	**PE-** Professional Engineer
DC- Chiropractor	**PH** -(suffix)- Pearl Harbor Survivor
DO- Osteopathic Doctor	**PH** -(prefix)- Purple Heart
DPM- Podiatrist	**QQ-** Historic
DS- Disabled Veteran	**R-** Street Rod, **RA-** Retired Air Force
EM- Emergency Medical Technician	**RI-** Rotary International
F- First Aider	**RU-** Rutgers University
FF- Firemans Mutual Benevolent Assoc.	**SS-** Silver Star
	SS- Submarine Veteran Silent Service
FP- Fraternal Order of Police	**SA -SZ** - Coastal protection
HA- HZ -Handicapped	**SD-** Square Dancer
IF- International Firefighters	**SG** - State Government
IM- Animal Friendly	**SH-** Seton Hall University
KI- Kiwanis International	**ST-** Stevens Tech
KC - Knights of Columbus	**US-** US Congress
MB- Freemason	**VFW-** Veteran of Foreign Wars
MD- Medical Doctor	**VV-** Vietnam Veteran
MG - Municipal Government	**WC-** Wildlife Conservation
	WV- VFW

Small numeric characters embossed on the right side of a plate indicates the number of plates issued to an individual or company on the same registration.

New Jersey does not designate county of origin or weight on license plates.

New Jersey Division of Motor Vehicle
CN 145, 225 East State St., Trenton, NJ 08666   Tel. 609-984-2354

NEW MEXICO

POLICE PATCH

DRIVERS LICENSE

PASSENGER PLATES

PASSENGER
1 PLATE 1 DECAL

PERSONALIZED

OPTIONAL
GRAPHIC

HANDICAPPED

STATE
SENATOR

ARMED
FORCES
RESERVES

GOVERNMENT

MOUNTED
PATROL

PURPLE HEART

AMATEUR
RADIO

INDIAN
TRIBAL
VEHICLE

NATIONAL
GUARD

TRUCK AND TRAILER PLATES

APPORTIONED

TRAILER

TRUCK WEIGHT
DISTANCE

PLATE VALIDATION

MO/YR

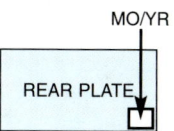

REAR PLATE

YEAR EXPIRE 00	YEAR EXPIRE 01

www.state.nm.us/state/htd.html

The "Land of Enchantment" issues one fully-reflectorized license plate. A county name decal appears at the top of most plates, and a "Zia" Indian sun-sign separates the numbers from letters and has been used continuously since 1927.

Distinctive captions:

MOUNTED PATROL - Statewide auxiliary police organization
NM RANGER - Auxiliary police organization
HORSELESS CARRIAGE - Vehicle at least 35 years old
DISABLED VETERAN - 100% disabled combat veteran

Codes:

Most recent issue New Mexico passenger and light truck plates are 3 numeric - 3 alpha. The county of origin name appears at the top of all (except official) new format plates, however this is no longer required by law.

Prefixes and suffixes indicate as follows:

A - Motorcycle
D - Dealer
DV - Disabled Veteran
F over **L** - Fleet registration
F over **T** - Freight trailer
G - Government
GM - Government motorcycle
HC - Horseless Carriage
HCM - Horseless Carriage motorcycle
HM - Handicapped motorcycle
H over **P** - Handicapped
I over **R** - Apportioned
KID- Children's Trust Fund

M over **H** - Manufactured home
MP - Mounted patrol
NG - National Guard
OF - Indian Tribal-owned
O over **H** - Off-Highway cycle
PB - Passenger bus
RR - New Mexico Ranger
R over **V** - Recreational vehicle
SBA - SBZ - School bus
T over **R** - Trailer
US - U.S. Govt.; Indian Agency
VET - Veteran
WDFT- Weight Distance Farm Truck
W over **D** - Weight distance

New Mexico does not indicate the weight of a vehicle on the license plate.

New Mexico Taxation & Revenue Department, Motor Vehicle Division
P.O.Box 1028, Santa Fe, NM 87594   Tel. 505-827- 2294

NEW YORK

POLICE PATCH

DRIVERS LICENSE

PASSENGER PLATES

PASSENGER
2 PLATES
WINDSHIELD DECAL

PERSONALIZED

DISABLED

ADRIONDACK REGION

NY CITY REGION

MUNICIPAL

STATE SENATE

CONSERVATION

SPECIAL PLATE NASCAR

SPECIAL PLATE SPORTS

STATE POLICE

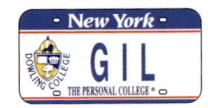

COLLEGIATE DOWLING

TRUCK AND TRAILER PLATES

APPORTIONED

COMMERCIAL

SEMI-TRAILER

74

YEAR EXPIRE 00	YEAR EXPIRE 01	
FRONT PLATE	REAR PLATE	WINDSHIELD VALIDATION	WINDSHIELD VALIDATION	www.nydmv.state.ny.us

The "Empire State" issues two fully-reflectorized license plates using several different numeric configurations. A windshield decal is issued for a two-year validation period. The Statue of Liberty can appear on the left side or in the center of the plate.

Distinctive captions:

COMMERCIAL - Vehicle used in commerce
FARM - Farm vehicle with restricted highway use
GOLD STAR MOTHER - Survivor of war casualty
LIVERY - Passenger vehicle for hire
(often a limousine)
OFFICIAL - Any government owned vehicle
TRACTOR - Power unit of a tractor trailer combination
T&LC - Non-medallion cabs and limousines in NY City.

TRAILER- All types of trailers including semi-trailers.
SCHOOL - Vehicle that belongs to a school system
SPEC-COMM - Special purpose equipment construction etc.
SURVIVORS OF THE SHIELD - Family of police killed on duty

Other captions found on New York plates:

AMBULANCE
AIR NATIONAL GUARD
ARMY NATIONAL GUARD
BUS
CONGRESS. MEDAL OF HONOR
CORONER
COUNTY LEGISLATOR
CITY COURT

CIVIL COURT
COUNTY CLERK
COUNTY COURT
COURT OF APPEALS
COURT OF CLAIMS
CRIMINAL COURT
DEALER
DISTRICT ATTORNEY
DISTRICT COURT
DISABLED VETERAN

FAMILY COURT
ENVIRON. CONS.
POLICE
FORMER PRISONER OF WAR
HISTORICAL
JSC APPELLATE DIV
MEDICAL EXAMINER
NAVAL MILITIA
NY ASSEMBLY

NY SENATE
NYC COUNCIL
STATE GUARD
SUPREME COURT
SURROGATE COURT
TAXI
TOW TRUCK
U.S. CONGRESS
U.S. SENATE
VAN POOL

Codes:

New York does not designate the county of origin or weight of a vehicle on regular plates. The following combinations are reserved for special groups:

AL (1-100) - American Legion officer
(1-9999) **DAV** (1-9999) - Disabled veteran
DCH (1-9999) - Chiropractor
(1-9999) **DDS** (1-9999) - Dr. Dental Surgery
DS (201-1000) - Dentist
(1-9999) **DV** - Paralyzed war veteran
(1-9999) **DPM**- Podiatrist
ED (1-9999)- Educator
(1-9999) **EMT** -Emergency Medical Technician.
(1-9999) **EMPT** - Emt paramedic
JUS (1-9) - Judge U.S. Customs Court
(1-20) **LBA** - Lieut. Benevolent Assn.
LBA (1-20) - Former Board member LBA
LCA (1-50) - Legislative correspondent
(1-9999) **LRT**- Licensed Radiology Technician.
2LU (2-999) - Limited use automobile
MD (1-99999) - Medical doctor
(1-99) **METRO** (1-99) - Metropol. Police Conf.
NYP - New York Press
NCAP (1-999) - Nassau County Aux. Police
NCPBA (1-99) - Nassau County PBA
(1-999) **OD** - Opthomologist dispenser

(1-9999) **PBA** (1-9999) - Police Ben. Assn.
PE (1-9999) - Professional engineer
PSY (1000-1999) - Psychologist
PT (1000-1999) - Physiotherapist
RCL (1-50) - Rockland County Supervisor
(1-9999) **RLC** (1-9999) - Rural letter carrier
(1-9999) **RN** (901-9999) - Registered nurse
RPA (1-9999) - Registered Physician's Assnt.
(1-9999) **RX** (1-9999)- Pharmacist
SBA (1-20) - Sgt. Benevolent Assn.
SFF (1-120) - State Firefighter Assn.
(1-9999) **SMA** (1-9999)- State Magistrate
(1-999) **TV** (1-999) - Television crew
UFA (1-9999) - Uniformed Fire Assn.
UPI (1-9999) - United Press
USALJ - U.S. Admin. Law Judge
USJ - Federal Court Judge
VA (1000-9999) - Dealer issued pass.plate
VAA (100-999) - Dealer issued comm. plate
VAS (100-999) - Volunteer ambulance service
VF (1-99999) - Volunteer fireman
(1-9999) **VFW** (1-9999) - Veterans of Fgn. Wars
ZAA-ZZZ (100-999) - Rental vehicle

New York Department of Motor Vehicles, Empire State Plaza
Albany NY 12228   Tel. 518-474-2121

NORTH CAROLINA

POLICE PATCH

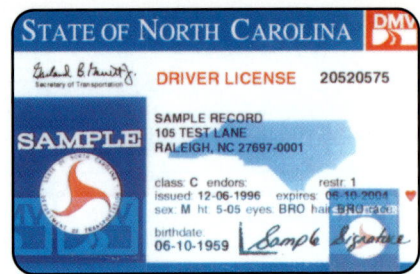

DRIVERS LICENSE

PASSENGER PLATES

PASSENGER
1 PLATE 1 DECAL

PERSONALIZED

HANDICAPPED

STATE OWNED

**COLLEGIATE
UNIV. OF NC**

**COLLEGIATE
NC STATE**

**STATE
OFFICIAL**

WILDLIFE

**SPECIAL
CAUSE
HATTERAS**

**NAVAL
RESERVE**

PURPLE HEART

TRANSPORTER

TRUCK AND TRAILER PLATES

**APPORTIONED
ANNUAL**

**APPORTIONED
PERMANENT**

TRUCK

**TRAILER
MULTI-YEAR**

PLATE VALIDATION

MONTH   YEAR

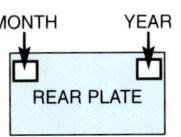

REAR PLATE

YEAR EXPIRE **00**

YEAR EXPIRE **01**

www.dmv.dot.state.nc.us

The "Tarheel State" issues one fully-reflectorized license plate. The last general re-issue was in 1980, so there are many older plates in use (some not reflectorized). Current plates are three alpha - four numeric while previous issues were three alpha- three numeric.

Distinctive captions:

FIRST IN FLIGHT- Commemorates the Wright brothers' flight at Kitty Hawk, NC
PERMANENT- Permanent plate issued to city and county-owned vehicles
HORSELESS CARRIAGE- Vehicle at least 50 years old
ANTIQUE- Collector's vehicle between 35 and 49 years old

Codes:

North Carolina issues 3 alpha - 4 numeric character plates to passenger vehicles. Trucks and other non-passenger vehicle plates have a 1 or 2 alpha prefix followed by numerics. Alpha prefix codes are as follows:

AAA - ZZZ	Regular passenger
AA - BF	Private truck 5000 lbs & up
A - E	Trailer
B	Shaw University
C	Clerk of the Superior Court
CAP	Civil Air Patrol
D	Duke University
DA	Dist. Atty. (# is district)
DOT	Dept. of Transportation
DV	Disabled veteran
E	East Carolina University
F	Wake Forest University
FA - FZ	Farm vehicle
FD	Franchised auto dealer
HC	Honorary Consul
HD	Handicapped driver
HP	Highway Patrol
ID	Independent auto dealer
J	Judiciary (numeric is district)
	1-19 Supreme Court and Appeals Court
	21-99 Superior Court (district plus 20)
	101-199 District Court Judge (dist +100)
	Suffix A- Additional Judge in district (Junior seniority)
L	Apportioned trailer

1-280	State Officials
LA-LF	Apportioned truck
M	5 year trailer plate
ME	Special mobile equipment
MF	Manufacturer
NC	National Guard
NR	Naval Reserve
P	(prefix or suffix) Permanent
P over D	Partially-disabled veteran
PX - PZ	State owned
POW	Former Prisoner of War
RA - RZ	Rental vehicle
RF	Rescue fireman
RS	Rescue
S	N.C. State University
SR	StreetRod
U	University of N.C.
USJ	Federal Judge (low number indicates seniority)
VF	Volunteer fireman
W over C	Wildlife Conservation
ZA	Drive-away
ZB - ZF	Common carrier, contract carrier, bus for hire

North Carolina does not designate county of origin or weight of vehicle on plates.

North Caroling of Motor Vehicle
1100 New Bern Ave., Raleigh, NC 27697   Tel. 919-733-2403

NORTH DAKOTA

POLICE PATCH

DRIVERS LICENSE

PASSENGER PLATES

PASSENGER
2 PLATES 1 DECAL
ON REAR

PERSONALIZED

HANDICAPPED

**STATE/CITY/
COUNTY
OWNED**

**AMATEUR
RADIO**

**DISABLED
VETERAN**

**ELECTED
OFFICIAL**

FORMER POW

**INDIAN TRIBE
CHIPPEWA**

**INDIAN TRIBE
SIOUX**

**INDIAN TRIBE
SPIRIT LAKE**

COLLECTOR

TRUCK AND TRAILER PLATES

APPORTIONED

TRAILED

**APPORTIONED
POWER UNIT**

PLATE VALIDATION

MO/YR

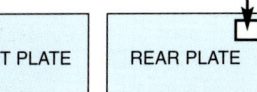

FRONT PLATE	REAR PLATE

YEAR EXPIRE 00	YEAR EXPIRE 01

www.state.nd.us.dot

The "Peace Garden State" issues two fully-reflectorized license plates. Most passenger plates are issued in the three alpha - three numeric format; however, low numbers 1 to 10,000 are also issued, as well as a new series prefixed by "ND".

Distinctive captions:

OFCL- State,city, county-owned vehicles
Peace Garden State - A park located on the Canadian border dedicated to peace
Pioneer- Collector's vehicle 40 years old restored to its original condition

Codes:

North Dakota issues 3 alpha-3 numeric character plates to regular passenger cars and trucks. These plates have no county or weight codes. Owners can request a specific number plate (between 7 - 10,000) which will be issued at no extra charge if available.

Special class vehicles have an alpha prefix :

DV - Disabled Veteran
FR - Auto manufacturer's rep.
E - State /city vehicle (tax exempt)
MH - Mobile home dealer
N - New car dealer
PR - Prorated vehicle

PT - Prorated trailer
SD - Semi-trailer dealer
T - Trailer
U - Used car dealer
DD - Dealer demonstrator
DX - Dealer in transit

Low numbers are issued to:

1 - State Governor
2 - Senior U.S. Senator
3 - Junior U.S. Senator
4 - U.S. Congressman

5 - Governor's second vehicle
6 - Lieutenant Governor
ND2 - Lt. Governor

Farm trucks can be distinguished by a red sticker on the plate.

North Dakota Department of Transportation, Motor Vehicle Division
608 East Boulevard Ave., Bismarck ND 58505-0780   Tel. 701- 328- 2725

OHIO

POLICE PATCH

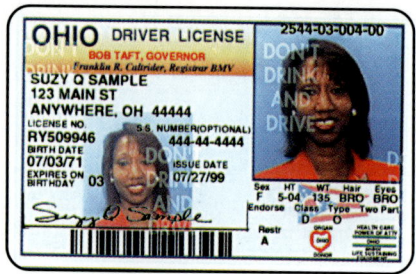

DRIVERS LICENSE

PASSENGER PLATES

PASSENGER

PERSONALIZED

PASSENGER
OLDER BASE

PASSENGER
RECENT BASE

HANDICAPPED

DISABLED
VETERAN

ENVIRONMENT

COLLEGIATE
OHIO STATE

COLLEGIATE
MIAMI UNIV.

NATIONAL
GUARD

WILDLIFE

COURT
ORDERED

TRUCK AND TRAILER PLATES

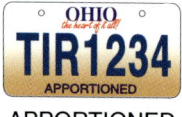

APPORTIONED

TRUCK

TRAILER

PLATE VALIDATION

MO/YR

YEAR EXPIRE 00	YEAR EXPIRE 01

FRONT PLATE

REAR PLATE

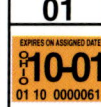

www.dot.state.oh.us/

The "Buckeye State" issues two fully-reflectorized license plates. Passenger plates are required to display a county name decal. A new series of graphic plates is presently being phased-in.

Distinctive captions:

C.A.P - Civil Air Patrol
COLLECTOR -Collectors item fair market value $100 or more
FARM BUS - Bus used exclusively to transport farm workers
GOVERNMENT- Vehicle owned by the Federal Government
HISTORICAL - Collector's vehicle at least 25 years old (Black on white)
HONORARY CONSUL - Foreign Consular Service (Honorary)
IN TRANSIT - Used to transport new and used vehicles
HOUSE VEH - House car, house trailer or travel trailer
NON-COMM - 3/4 ton or less capacity, non-profit use
PURPLE HEART - Veteran who was wounded in combat
RADIO - Owner of a broadcast radio station
SPECIAL - Plate used to road test motor vehicles by a non-motor vehicle dealer
TELEVISION - Commercial TV station owner
VOITURE - U.S. service organization vehicle used in parades
VETERAN - Disabled veteran
SENIOR - Bus used to transport persons 65 years of age or older

Codes:

Most passenger car plates have 3 alpha- 3 numeric characters divided by an outline of the state. The county name appears on a decal at the bottom of the plate. There are no county codes on Ohio license plates.

Ohio has a special red on yellow plate that is issued by a court order to the family of a vehicle owner who has lost the privilege to drive. Known as a "Family Plate", it permits other members of the family to operate the vehicle during the term of the suspension.

Reserved plates contain three or fewer letters, a combination of letters and numbers, or numbers alone. These plates are available for an additional $10 yearly fee.

Ohio Bureau of Motor Vehicles
4300 Kimberly Parkway, PO Box 16520, Columbus, OH 43266-0020
Tel. 614-752-7100   1-800-589-TAGS

OKLAHOMA

POLICE PATCH

DRIVERS LICENSE

PASSENGER PLATES

PASSENGER
1 PLATE 2 DECALS

PASSENGER
OLDER BASE

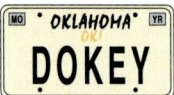

PERSONALIZED

DISABLED

TRIBAL
VEHICLE

COLLEGIATE
PAN HANDLE
UNIV.

IWO JIMA
VETERAN

ROUTE 66
ASSOCIATION

OLYMPIC
SPIRIT

NATIVE
HERITAGE

ENVIRONMENT

HEARTLAND

TRUCK AND TRAILER PLATES

APPORTIONED

TRUCK
OLDER ISSUE

COMMERCIAL
TRUCK

TRAILER NON
EXPIRE

PLATE VALIDATION

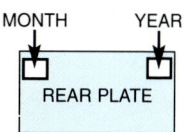

MONTH   YEAR

REAR PLATE

YEAR EXPIRE 00
2000

YEAR EXPIRE 01
2001

www.oktax.state.ok.us

The "Sooner State" issues one fully-reflectorized license plate. Oklahoma has not had a general plate re-issue since 1979 and there are four different bases currently in use. The first letters on the passenger plate are a county code. Personalized plates are available in a choice of six different background colors.

Distinctive captions:

ANTIQUE - Vehicle 30 years or older used for historical exhibition
E - Tax exempt (publicly-owned vehicle)
INTRANSIT - Vehicle hauling for hire (i.e. prefab. houses)
TRIBAL VEH. - Vehicle owned by Indian tribe

Codes:

Oklahoma issues 3 alpha -3 numeric plates to passenger vehicles. Older plates still in use have a 2 alpha county code prefix:

AD - Adair (Stillwell)
AL - Alfalfa (Cherokee)
AT - Atoka (Atoka)
BV - Beaver (Beaver)
BK, BE - Beckham (Sayre)
BL - Blaine (Watonga)
BR, CY - Bryan (Durant)
CA, CD - Caddo (Anadarko)
CN, CNN, CX, CXX - Canadian (El Reno)
CR, CRR, CE - Carter (Ardmore)
CW - Choctaw (Hugo)
CI - Cimarron (Boise City)
CL, CLL, CV, CY, CF, CYY
CVV - Cleveland (Norman)
CO - Coal (Colgate)
CB, CC, CH, CM, CP, CCB - Comanche (Lawton)
CT - Cotton (Walters)
CG - Craig (Vinita)
CJ, CK, CKK - Creek (Sapulpa)
CS, CSS - Custer (Arapaho)

Other codes:

D - Dealer
KIA - Unremarried spouse of person killed in action
H - Okla. House of Rep.
HD - Disabled person

CZ,CZZ- Cherokee (Tahlequah)
DL, DE - Delaware (Jay)
DW - Dewey (Taloga)
EL - Ellis (Arnett)
GA, GR, GF, GB - Garfield (Enid)
GN, GV- Garvin (Pauls Vly)
GD, GY- Grady (Chksha.)
GT - Grant (Medford)
GE - Greer (Mangum)
HM - Harmon (Hollis)
HP - Harper (Buffalo)
HK - Haskell (Stigler)
HG - Hughes (Holdenville)
JA, JK, JS, JX - Jackson (Altus)
JE - Jefferson (Waurika)
JN - Johnson (Tishomingo)
KA, KK,KY ,KAY- Newkirk (Kay)
KF - Kingfisher (Kingfisher)
KW - Kiowa (Hobart)
LA - Latimer (Wilburton)
LE, LF - LeFlore (Poteau)
LN, LL - Lincoln (Chandler)

LG, LO - Logan (Guthrie)
LV - Love (Marietta)
ML, MN - McClain (Purcell)
MC, MT- McCurtain (Idabel)
MO - McIntosh (Eufaula)
MA- Major (Fairview)
MR - Marshall (Madill)
ME, MY - Mayes (Pryor)
MU - Murray (Sulphur)
MG, MK, MS, MB - Muskogee (Muskogee)
NB - Noble (Perry)
NW - Nowata (Nowata)
OK - Okfuskee (Okemah)
OL, OM - Okmulgee (Okmulgee)
OA, OE, OG, OS - Osage (Pawhuska)
OT, OW - Ottawa (Miami)
PW - Pawnee (Pawnee)
PA, PY, PF Payne(Stillwater)
PB, PS - Pittsburg(McAlester)
PC, PN - Pontotoc (Ada)
PE, PT, PD, PTT- Pottawatomie (Shawnee)
PM - Pushmataha (Antlers)

POW - Former prisoner of war
S - Oklahoma state senate
T - Commercial truck
TRB - Tribal-owned vehicle
V - Motor home

RM - Roger Mills (Cheynn.)
RG, RE, RO - Rogers (Claremore)
SE, SM - Seminole(Wewoka)
SH-SY - Sequoyah(Sallisaw)
SN,SP,ST- Stephens(Duncan
TX, TS - Texas (Guymon)
TL - Tillman (Frederick)
WG, WN - Wagoner (Wagoner)
WA, WH, WS, WI - Washington (Bartlesville)
WT - Washita (Cordell)
WD -Woods (Alva)
WB,WW, WE - Woodward (Woodward)
XA - XZ (except I &Q) - Oklahoma County (Okla Cty)
YA -YS (except I)-Okla. County (Okla. City)
ZA - ZZ (except I&Q) Tulsa (Tulsa)
ZZA - ZZG - Tulsa (Tulsa)

Oklahoma does not designate the weight of a vehicle on the license plate.

Oklahoma Tax Commission, Motor Vehicle Division
2501 N. Lincoln Boulevard, Oklahoma City. OK 73194   Tel. 405-521-2510   83

OREGON

POLICE PATCH

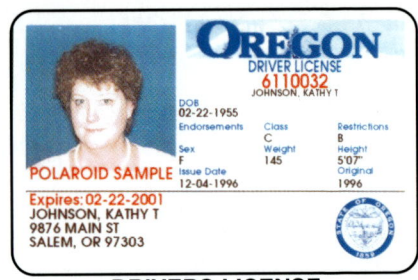

DRIVERS LICENSE

PASSENGER PLATES

PASSENGER
2 PLATES 2 DECAL
ON BOTH

PASSENGER
OLDER BASE

PERSONALIZED

PASSENGER
OLDER BASE

DISABLED
VETERAN

OREGON TRAIL
ASSOCIATION

ELECTED
OFFICIAL

SALMON

NATIONAL
GUARD

DEALER

TRUCK AND TRAILER PLATES

APPORTIONED

HEAVY TRUCK
APPORTIONED

TRUCK

LIGHT TRUCK
APPORTIONED

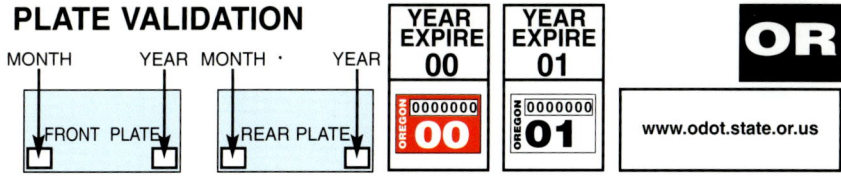

PLATE VALIDATION

MONTH   YEAR MONTH ·   YEAR

FRONT PLATE   REAR PLATE

YEAR EXPIRE 00

YEAR EXPIRE 01

OREGON 0000000 00

OREGON 0000000 01

www.odot.state.or.us

OR

The "Pacific Wonderland" issues two fully-reflectorized license plates. Oregon has not had a general plate re-issue since 1955, and there are seven different bases currently in use. Oregon registers motor vehicles for a two-year period, and has the lowest registration fees in the nation. A special Oregon Trail commemorative plate is available for an additional $5 fee.

Distinctive captions:

ANTIQUE VEHICLE - Collector's vehicle at least half the age of the auto industry which began in 1900
PERMANENT FLEET - Vehicle registered as part of a fleet
PUBLICLY OWNED - State, city, county government-owned vehicles (Includes Indian tribal govt.-owned vehicles.)

Codes:

Oregon issues 3 alpha - 3 numeric plates to passenger cars. There are no county of origin   codes in the numbering system. Several older issue passenger bases with different color combinations are still valid for use.

All truck, trailer, bus and other non-passenger car plates have
an alpha prefix followed by numerics.
The prefix codes are as follows:

A over **Q** - Antique
B   - Bus
C over **N** - Charity/non-profit trk, bus   **D** over **A** - Oregon dealer
E   - Publicly-owned vehicle
F   - Farm vehicle
F over **R** - For-rent trailer
H   - Motor home
H over **F** - Fixed load (over 3,000 lbs)
H over **P** - Heavy trailer (permanent)
H over **T** - Heavy trailer

K   - Camper
L over **F** - Light fixed load (- 3,000 lbs)
L over **T** - Light trailer
N over **G** - National Guard
P over **W** - Former Prisoner of War
R   -Travel trailer
S over **P** - Special-interest vehicle (25 years old)
T   -Truck
T over **W** - Tow Truck
TR   -Transporter
U   - Utility trailer

Oregon does not indicate the weight of a vehicle on license plates.

Oregon Department of Transportation, Driver and Motor Vehicle Services
1905 Lana Ave. NE, Salem ,OR 97314   Tel. 503-945-5118

PENNSLYVANIA

POLICE PATCH

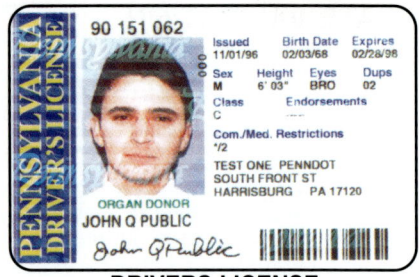

DRIVERS LICENSE

PASSENGER PLATES

**PASSENGER
NEW BASE**
1 PLATE 1 DECAL

PASSENGER
1 PLATE 1 DECAL

PASSENGER
1 PLATE 1 DECAL

PERSONALIZED

**WILDLIFE
OTTER**

**WILDLIFE
PA ZOO**

**ENVIRONMENT
OWL**

**RAILROAD
HERITAGE**

**COLLEGIATE
PENN STATE
ALUMNI**

CMH

DARE

PURPLE HEART

TRUCK AND TRAILER PLATES

APPORTIONED

**COMMERCIAL
TRUCK**

TRAILER

**APPORTIONED
TRUCK OLDER
BASE**

PLATE VALIDATION

MO/YR

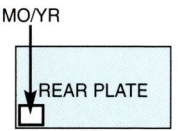

↓REAR PLATE

YEAR EXPIRE **00**

YEAR EXPIRE **01**

www.dot.state.pa.us
(vehicle services)

The "Keystone State" issues one partially-reflectorized (glass beads on paint) license plate. Pennsylvania has not had a general plate re-issue since 1977 and there are three different bases in use. When vehicles are first registered all plates are issued with a decal containing only the letter "T" indicating temporary registration.

Distinctive captions:

ANTIQUE - Collector's vehicle 25 years or older
CLASSIC CAR - Exhibition vehicle 10 years or older and a discontinued model
HEARING IMPAIRED - Driver with special limited hearing condition
HUSBANDRY - Farm vehicle with limited highway use
KEYSTONE STATE - Commemorates Pennsylvania's "keystone" position in the center of the original thirteen colonies
STREET ROD - Modified exhibition vehicle built in 1948 or earlier

PP - Press photographer **PA** - State Senator **HR** - Pa. House of Rep.

Codes:

Regular passenger plates have 6 or 7 characters: all numeric, 3 alpha - 4 numeric, 3 alpha - 3 numeric, 1 alpha -5 numeric, 3 alpha- numeric (alpha rotates and can be found in all positions).

The following alpha and numeric combinations are reserved for special use:

1, 2	- Governor and Lt. Gov.	**HP**	- Handicapped person
2 - 23	- Governor's cabinet	**MC**	- Member of Congress
24 - 999	- State officials	**MG** (prefix or suffix)	- Municipal Govt.
DV	- Disabled veteran	**PA** (10000 - 99999)	- State-owned.
EV	- Emergency vehicle	**PA** (1-50)	- Pa. Senate
FF	- Firefighter	**PA** (51-99)	- Pa. Senate retired
FD	- Fire Department	**PP**	- Press photographer
(1-255) **HR** (1 -225)	- Pa. House of Rep.	**USC** (1-25)	- U.S. Congress
		USS (1-4)	- U.S. Senate

Dealer plates have 7 characters and the alpha indicates the type:
A - New car **B** - Used car **C** - **MV** business   **MPD** - Moped   **MCD** - Motorcycle

Commercial vehicle, tractor, taxi, bus and trailer plates have 7 characters and the following alpha prefixes indicate the class of vehicle:

AA - AZ - Apportioned truck
BA - Bus
HC - HD - Motor home
IMP - Implement of husbandry (farm)
M over **T** - Mass transit
SA - SB - School bus

TA - TZ - Trailer
SME - Special mobile equipment
TX - Taxi
WR- Wildlife Resources
YA -YZ, CA - CZ (suffix or prefix) - Truck

Pennsylvania does not indicate county of origin or weight of a vehicle on plates.

**Pennsylvania Department of Transportation, Bureau of Motor Vehicles
River Front Office Center, 3rd Floor, 1101 South Front St.
Harrisburg, PA 17104- 2516
Tel. 717- 783 - 6517**

RHODE ISLAND

POLICE PATCH

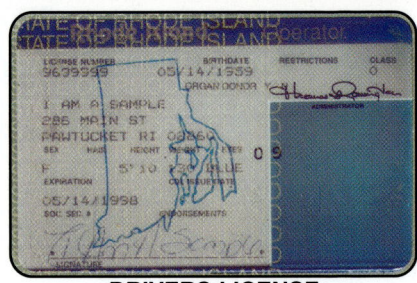

DRIVERS LICENSE

PASSENGER PLATES

PASSENGER
2 PLATES 1 DECAL
ON BOTH

PERSONALIZED

**OPTIONAL
GRAPHIC**

WAR VETERAN

STATE OWNED

**FOR HIRE
VEHICLE**

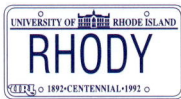

**COLLEGIATE
UNIV. OF RI**

ANTIQUE

TRUCK AND TRAILER PLATES

APPORTIONED

COMMERCIAL

TRAILER

JITNEY

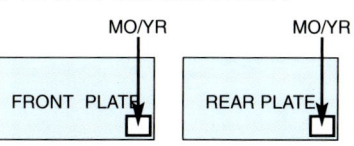

		YEAR EXPIRE 00	YEAR EXPIRE 01	
MO/YR	MO/YR			
FRONT PLATE	REAR PLATE			www.dot.state.ri.us

The "Ocean State" state issues two fully-reflectorized license plates. Rhode Island passenger plates are all numeric, or one or two alpha followed by numerics. Plates are re-validated for two-year periods. A new general-issue graphic "wave" plate was introduced October 1, 1996 and will eventually replace all previous base plates.

Distinctive captions:

ANTIQUE - Collector's vehicle 25 years or older
BAILEE - Repossessor
CITY- City-owned vehicle
COMM - Commercial vehicle (truck)
FARM - Farm vehicle with limited highway use
JITNEY - Bus plate last manufactured in 1968 but still in use
MOTOR VEHICLE REGISTRY - Plates issued to the Registrar
 of Motor Vehicles, his deputies and inspectors
NEWS PHOTOG - News photographer accredited in Rhode Island
PUBLIC - Motor vehicle for hire
STATE - State-owned vehicle
SUB - Station wagons
TOWN - Vehicle owned by a town
VETERAN - Disabled veteran
HANDICAPPED PARKING PLACARD - The wheelchair symbol is used
(Dashboard placard can be transferred to any vehicle used by the disabled person)

Codes:

Rhode Island passenger car plates are all numeric (1-99999) or 1-2 alpha followed by 1-3 numeric (A-1 through AA-123). Registrations are for a two-year period. The only other type vehicles issued passenger type plates are vans with windows all-around and passenger seating (not cargo vans). Pickup trucks receive commercial plates. Passenger plates are renewed on a schedule which corresponds to the first letter of the owners last name.

Trucks and other commercial vehicle plates are all numeric and clearly captioned. Rhode Island does not issue apportioned, tractor or handicapped license plates.

There are no county of origin, weight or use codes on Rhode Island plates. The majority of plates are issued for multi-year use. Dealer and transporter plates are replaced annually with a different color scheme.

Rhode Island Division of Motor Vehicles
286 Main Street, Pawtucket, RI 02860   Tel. 401- 277 -2970

SOUTH CAROLINA

POLICE PATCH

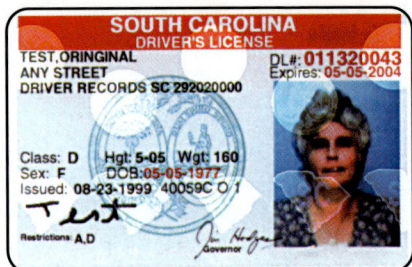

DRIVERS LICENSE

PASSENGER PLATES

PASSENGER
1 PLATE 2 DECALS

PERSONALIZED

**DISABLED
VETERAN**

**PEARL
HARBOR**

**COLLEGIATE
CLEMSON**

**COLLEGIATE
UNIV. OF SC.**

ENVIRONMENT

WILDLIFE

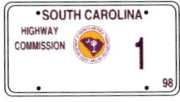

**HIGHWAY
COMMISSION**

PURPLE HEART

TRUCK AND TRAILER PLATES

APPORTIONED

TRUCK

**PERMANENT
TRAILER**

TRAILER

PLATE VALIDATION

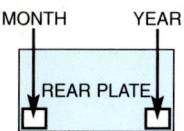

MONTH   YEAR

REAR PLATE

www.dot.state.sc.us

The "Palmetto State" issues one fully-reflectorized license plate. Next to Illinois, South Carolina issues the second largest variety of plates. Personalized and other special interest plates have a graphic design different from regular passenger plates.

Distinctive captions:

ANTIQUE AUTO - Collector's vehicle 30 years or older
EMT - Emergency medical technician
FARM - Vehicle used exclusively for farm and related industry
M/R DEALER - Manufacturer's repossession plate
RESCUE - Rescue vehicle
U.S. MIL. RES - Member of active military reserve unit
UTILITY - Utility trailer
WHOLESALER - Wholesale automobile dealer

Codes:

South Carolina issues 3 alpha - 3 numeric graphic design plates to private passenger and light trucks for multi-year use.

Personalized plates have a different graphic design than the regular passenger plates. This personalized design is used for 138 different special group plates such as: State officials, educators, board members, and Miss South Carolina. These special plates, similar to personalized, are re-validated annually by decals.

State,city, county,regional and municipal government plates and certain veteran's plates are permanent and these also have a graphic background design showing the state seal.

The prefixes on this plate design have special meaning :

CG	County Government	**RG**	Regional Government
MG	Municipal Government	**SG**	State Government
POW	Ex-Prisoner of War	**V**	Disabled veteran

State officials are assigned the following plates:

1 - Governor	**4** - Treasurer	**7** - Dept. of Education
2 - Lt. Governor	**5** - Comptroller General	**8** - Adjutant General
3 - Sec. of State	**6** - Attorney General	**9** - Dept. of Agriculture

Trucks and trailers are issued new non-graphic plates each year. Other commercial vehicle plates are re-validated by decal. These plates have a 1 or 2 alpha prefix followed by numerics. The following alpha prefixes have special meaning:

CC (suffix) - Common Carrier	**SM** - Special mobile equipment
HT - House trailer	**TL** - Interstate trailer
P - Truck	**XX** - Dealer
PS - Semi-annual truck registration	**WX** - Wholesale dealer

South Carolina does not indicate the county of origin on plates.

S.C. Department of Revenue, Division of Motor Vehicles
P.O.Box 1498, Columbia, SC 29216 - 0008   Tel. 803-737- 1153

SOUTH DAKOTA

POLICE PATCH

DRIVERS LICENSE

PASSENGER PLATES

PASSENGER
2 PLATES 1 DECAL
ON BOTH

PASSENGER
2 PLATES 1 DECAL
ON BOTH

HANDICAPPED

**DISABLED
VETERAN**

**CITY/COUNTY
OWNED**

FIREFIGHTER

**NATIONAL
GUARD**

FORMER POW

**INDIAN TRIBE
CROW CREEK**

**INDIAN TRIBE
LOWER BRULE**

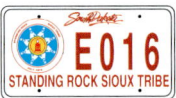

**INDIAN TRIBE
STANDING
ROCK**

**ORGANIZATION
PLATE**

TRUCK AND TRAILER PLATES

APPORTIONED

COMMERCIAL

**APPORTIONED
TRAILER**

PLATE VALIDATION

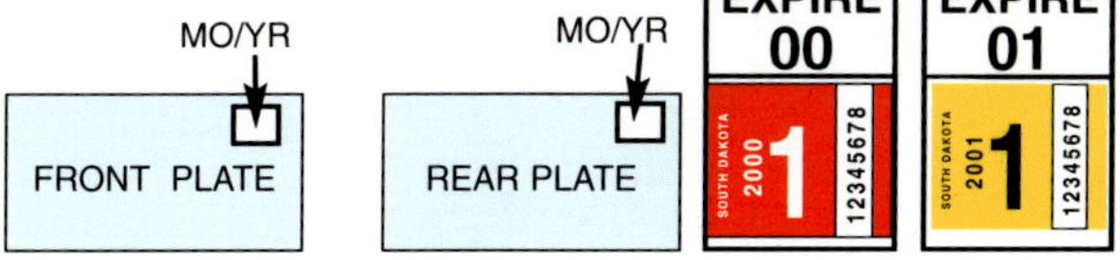

MO/YR — FRONT PLATE

MO/YR — REAR PLATE

YEAR EXPIRE 00	YEAR EXPIRE 01
SOUTH DAKOTA 2000 1 12345678	SOUTH DAKOTA 2001 1 12345678

SD

www.state.sd.us

The "Home of Mount Rushmore" issues two fully-reflectorized plates. The prefix on each passenger plate is a county code.

Distinctive captions:

CONSTR - Construction equipment
HISTORICAL-Collector's vehicle at least 30 years old
TAX EXEMPT - State, county, city, non-profit training centers, school and tribal vehicles
GREAT FACES - Promotional slogan for Mount Rushmore monument

Codes:

South Dakota passenger plates have 7 characters.
The code and county (county seats) are as follows:

1 Minnehaha (Sioux Falls)
2 Pennington (Rapid City)
3 Brown (Aberdeen)
4 Beadle (Huron)
5 Codington (Watertown)
6 Brookings (Brookings)
7 Yankton (Yankton)
8 Davison (Mitchell)
9 Lawrence (Deadwood)
10 Aurora (Plankinton)
11 Bennett (Martin)
12 Bon Homme (Tyndall)
13 Brule (Chamberlain)
14 Buffalo (Gannvalley)
15 Butte (Belle Fourche)
16 Campbell (Mound City)
17 Charles Mix (Lake Andes)
18 Clark (Clark)
19 Clay (Vermillion)
20 Corson (McIntosh)
21 Custer (Custer)
22 Day (Webster)
23 Deuel (Clear Lake)
24 Dewey (Timber Lake)

25 Douglas (Armour)
26 Edmunds (Ipswich)
27 Fall River (Hot Springs)
28 Faulk (Faulkton)
29 Grant (Milbank)
30 Gregory (Burke)
31 Haakon (Philip)
32 Hamlin (Hayti)
33 Hand (Miller)
34 Hanson (Alexandria)
35 Harding (Buffalo)
36 Hughes (Pierre)
37 Hutchinson (Olivet)
38 Hyde (Highmore)
39 Jackson (Kadoka)
40 Jerauld (Wessington Sprgs.)
41 Jones (Murdo)
44 Kingsbury (De Smet)
43 Lake (Madison)
44 Lincoln (Canton)
45 Lyman (Kennebec)
46 McCook (Salem)
47 McPherson (Leola)
48 Marshall (Britton)

49 Meade (Sturgis)
50 Mellette (White River)
51 Miner (Howard)
52 Moody (Flandreau)
53 Perkins (Bison)
54 Potter (Gettysburg)
55 Roberts (Sisseton)
56 Sanborn (Woonsocket)
57 Spink (Redfield)
58 Stanley (Fort Pierre)
59 Sully (Onida)
60 Tripp (Winner)
61 Turner (Parker)
62 Union (Elk Point)
63 Walworth (Selby)
64 Ziebach (Dupree)
65 Shannon (*Wounded Knee)
66 Yankton (Yankton)
67 Todd (Mission)
65,67 Are entirely within native American reservations
77 Dealer plate

Commercial vehicles are issued multi-year plates.The characters are 1 alpha -4 numeric and the year and ton weight class appears on the validation decal.

South Dakota tax-exempt plates are issued to state, city, county and tribal-owned vehicles.

The following alpha prefix codes are used:

CO - County-owned
CY - City-owned
GFP - Game, Fish, Park Dept.

HP - Highway Patrol
SC, ED - School vehicles
DE - Driver's education

South Dakota Department of Revenue, Division of Motor Vehicles
118 West Capitol Avenue, Pierre, SD 57501-2080
Tel. 605-773-3545

TENNESSEE

POLICE PATCH

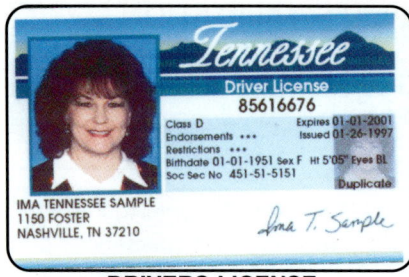

DRIVERS LICENSE

PASSENGER PLATES

PASSENGER

PASSENGER
OLDER BASE

DISABLED
VETERAN

PERSONALIZED

STATE SENATE

STATE
GOVERNMENT

STATE
VEHICLE

COLLEGIATE
UNIV. OF TN

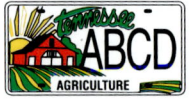

AGRICULTURE

SMOKY MTN
NTL. PARK

SQUARE
DANCE

WALKING
HORSE

TRUCK AND TRAILER PLATES

TRUCK
APPORTIONED

SEMI-TRAILER

TRUCK

PLATE VALIDATION

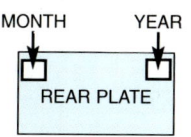

MONTH   YEAR

REAR PLATE

YEAR EXPIRE	YEAR EXPIRE
00	**01**

www.state.tn.us

The "Volunteer State" issues one fully-reflectorized license plate. The county of origin appears on a decal at the bottom of each passenger plate. Many counties impose a wheel tax and require a decal on the plate.

Distinctive captions:

ANTIQUE - Vehicle at least 25 years old
EMERGENCY- Emergency services including ham radio operators
GOV'T SERVICE - Government-owned vehicle
JOINT - Plate issued to both farm and semi-commercial vehicle

Codes:

Private passenger vehicle plates are 3 numeric - 3 alpha and the county name appears on the plate. Some counties have a wheel tax, and a decal on the lower right indicates payment.

Annual plates are issued to special classes of passenger cars. Most plates are clearly captioned, and the following can be recognized by the alpha prefix code:

GA - GZ - City, county, govt. vehicle   **TX** - Taxi
MUS   - Music City (private bus   **USJ** - Federal Judge
               owned by an entertainer)   **1**   - Governor
S   - State govt. vehicle   **1X** - Former governor

Trucks and other commercial vehicles are issued plates with a 2 alpha prefix code. Up until 1989 they were issued new plates yearly, currently they are revalidated by a decal. The first alpha indicates class, the second is a weight code. Each class has its own second alpha weight code:

First alpha(s)   Class

P - Private
H - For hire
M - Moving van (household)
S - Joint (Semi-comm. farm)
WD - Well-driller
FL - Fixed load
BA - Bus (unlimited operation)
BB - BD   - Bus (limited area)

Second alpha(s) (Maximum Gross Wgt)

This is the weight code for private trucks

AA - BZ	9,000 lbs.
M - MZ	16,000
P - PZ	20,000
R - RZ	26,000
S	32,000
T	38,000
U	44,000
V	56,000
W	66,000
XY	80,000

Semi-trailer plates are 1 alpha - 5 numeric. Apportioned plates have an alpha suffix.

Tennessee Department of Revenue, Motor Vehicle Commission
Titling & Registration Division, 44 Vantage Way, Suite 160
Nashville,TN 37243   Tel. 615-401-6851

TEXAS

POLICE PATCH

DRIVERS LICENSE

PASSENGER PLATES

PASSENGER
2 PLATES

PASSENGER
150 YRS
STATEHOOD

PASSENGER
1990 ISSUE

PASSENGER
1996 ISSUE

PASSENGER
1985 ISSUE

PERSONAIZED

NATIONAL
GUARD

FIREFIGHTER

COLLEGIATE
SW TEX UNIV.

FORESTRY

DISABLED
PERSONALIZED

HAM AMATEUR
RADIO

TRUCK AND TRAILER PLATES

TRUCK
APPORTIONED

TRUCK

TRAILER

WINDSHIELD VALIDATION

YEAR EXPIRE 00	YEAR EXPIRE 01

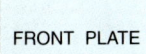

FRONT PLATE	REAR PLATE	WINDSHIELD VALIDATION	WINDSHIELD VALIDATION	www.dot.state.tx.us

The "Lone Star State" issues two fully-reflectorized plates. Starting in 1995 a windshield decal has been used for vehicle validation and many plates continue expiration decal on the rear license plate.

Distinctive captions:

ANTIQUE - Collector's vehicle at least 25 years old
COMBINATION - Truck or tractor over 1 ton in use with a semi-trailer over 6000 lbs.
CONSULAR OFFICIAL - Honorary position representing foreign government
CONSERVATION- Soil conservation equipment
DISASTER - Disaster relief vehicle operated by non-profit organization
EXEMPT- State or municipal-owned vehicle
MACHINERY - Water drilling or construction equipment
PERMIT - Oil well equipment for highway use
TEST CAR - Plate used by manufacturer to test new vehicles
TOKEN TRAILER - Semi-trailer over 6,000 lbs pulled by tractor with a
combination plate

Codes:

Regular passenger plates are 3 numeric - 3 alpha, and 3 alpha-2 numeric -1 alpha.

Texas does not use county of origin or weight codes on their plates.

The county of origin can be traced by the small 6 - digit serial number printed on the validation decals which are issued annually by the tax collectors in each of the 254 Texas counties. Truck, trailer and commercial plates have 6 characters with various alpha numeric combinations.

Texas issues over 1 million special license plates in 88 categories.

Texas Department of Transportation, Vehicle Titles and Registration Division
4000 Jackson Avenue, Austin TX 78779-0001   Tel. 512-302-2076

UTAH

POLICE PATCH

DRIVERS LICENSE

PASSENGER PLATES

**PASSENGER
2 PLATES
REAR DECALS**

**PASSENGER
CENTENNIAL**

PERSONALIZED

DISABLED

**HIGHWAY
PATROL**

**NATIONAL
GUARD**

WILDLIFE

DEALER

MANUFACTURER

COLLECTOR

**PEARL
HARBOR
VET**

SNOWMOBILER

TRUCK AND TRAILER PLATES

**TRUCK
APPORTIONED**

TRUCK

TRAILER

PLATE VALIDATION

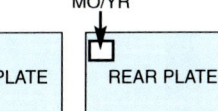

MO/YR

FRONT PLATE   REAR PLATE

YEAR EXPIRE 00

YEAR EXPIRE 01

www.sr.ex.state.ut.us

The "Beehive State" issues two fully-reflectorized plates. Utah has not had a general plate re-issue since 1973 and there are four different bases currently in use. A county decal (with a two letter abbreviation) is required to be displayed in the upper left corner of most plates.

Distinctive captions:

HORSELESS CARRIAGE - Vehicle at least 30 years old
RADIO - F.C.C. licensed amateur radio operator

Codes:

Utah issues 3 numeric- 3 alpha character plates to private passenger vehicles. The numbering system is for individual vehicle identification only. County of origin appears on a 2 alpha decal applied to the upper left corner of the plate.Colorful graphic statehood centennial plates are available for an additional fee and are issued in the 3 numeric- 3 alpha series.

The counties and (county seats) are as follows:

BV - Beaver (Beaver)
BE - Box Elder (Brigham City)
CA - Cache (Logan)
CC - Carbon (Price)
DG - Daggett (Manila)
DA - Davis (Farmington)
DU - Duchesne (Duchesne)
EM - Emery (Castle Dale)
GA - Garfield (Panguitch)
GR - Grand (Moab)

RN - Iron (Parowan)
JU - Juab (Nephi)
KA - Kane (Kanab)
MD - Millard (Fillmore)
MN - Morgan (Morgan)
PT - Piute (Junction)
RH - Rich (Randolph)
SL - Salt Lake (Salt Lake City)
SJ - San Juan (Monticello)
SP - Sanpete (Manti)

SE - Sevier (Richfield)
SU - Summit (Coalville)
TE - Tooele (Tooele)
UN - Uintah (Vernal)
UT - Utah (Provo)
WA - Wasatch (Heber City)
WN - Washington (St. George)
WE - Wayne (Loa)
WB - Weber (Ogden)

Trucks, truck-tractors, trailers, buses and certain other non-passenger vehicles are issued multi-year graphic base plates with a 1-3 alpha prefix or suffix.

The alpha codes are as follows:

A - B   Trailers over 750 lbs. unladen
DL   Dealer
FA - FB   Farm vehicle
TN   Transporter

LW - LN   Truck, bus, taxi
MFG   Manufacturer
WK   Wrecker

Government owned vehicles have a (prefix or suffix) **EX**- meaning tax-exempt. Low numbers are assigned as:
1- Governor, **EX 2** - Lt.Governor, **EX3** - State Treasurer, **EX4** - State Auditor

Utah does not designate the county of origin, weight class or use restrictions on commercial-vehicle plates.

Utah State Tax Commission, Motor Vehicle Customer Service Division
210 North 1950 West, Salt Lake City, UT 84134   Tel. 801-297-3543

VERMONT

POLICE PATCH

DRIVERS LICENSE

PASSENGER PLATES

PASSENGER

PERSONALIZED

HANDICAPPED

ENVIRONMENT

SHERIFF

MUNICIPAL

FIREMAN

NATIONAL
GUARD

PEARL
HARBOR

HAM RADIO

PURPLE HEART

DEALER

TRUCK AND TRAILER PLATES

TRUCK
APPORTIONED

TRAILER

TRUCK

INTERSTATE
TRUCK
SPECIAL WGT.

PLATE VALIDATION

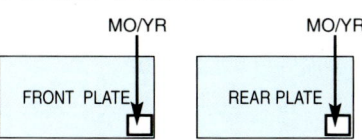

MO/YR   MO/YR

FRONT PLATE

REAR PLATE

YEAR EXPIRE 00

EXPIRES LAST DAY OF
JAN 00
0002751

YEAR EXPIRE 01

EXPIRES LAST DAY OF
JAN 01
0002751

VT

www.aot.state.vt.us/dmv

The "Green Mountain State" issues two fully-reflectorized plates. All regular passenger plates issued since 1990 are three alpha- three numeric. Earlier configurations are still in use.

Distinctive captions:

ACD - Auction car dealer
AGR - Farm truck
ANTIQUE - Vehicle 25 years old
ATV - All terrain vehicle (small plate)
CONTRACTOR - Contractor trailer
EXHIBIT - Exhibition vehicle
EX POW - Former prisoner of war
DLF - Farm machine dealer
FCD - Finance car dealer
DLH - Highway building equip. dealer

(Prefix) **DE** - Driver education vehicle
DLT - Trailer dealer
HUP - Truck highway use permit
MUN - Municipal-owned vehicle
NCD - New car dealer
SPECIAL PURPOSE - Const. equipment
TRA - Trailer
TRK - Truck
UCD - Used car dealer
VOL - Volunteer fire company

Codes:

Passenger car plates:
All regular passenger car plates issued since 1990 are 3 alpha - 3 numeric. Earlier configurations still in use are :

all numeric (1-9999)
alpha - numeric format:
1A123
123A4
1AA23
12AA3

Alphas **I, J, O, Q,U, V, Z** are not used as serial letters on Vermont plates.

Low numbers: (1- 99) are assigned by the Governor's office.
100-999 **VT** are assigned to state board members and appointees.
Plates are valid only for the term of office.

Trucks and commercial vehicles:
Various alpha numeric configurations are used. The vehicle class is designated by a caption or decal. Vermont does not designate the county of origin or the weight of a vehicle on license plates.

Vermont Agency of Transportation, Department of Motor Vehicles
120 State Street, Montpelier,VT 05603-0001   Tel. 802-828-2020

VIRGINIA

POLICE PATCH

DRIVERS LICENSE

PASSENGER PLATES

PASSENGER
2 DECALS
2 PLATES

PASSENGER
OLDER BASE

PERSONALIZED

HERITAGE
PLATE

CHESAPEAKE
BAY

OPTIONAL
GRAPHIC

PATRIOT

STATE VEHICLE

LIONS CLUB

COLLEGIATE

JAMESTOWN

WILDLIFE

TRUCK AND TRAILER PLATES

APPORTIONED
TRUCK

TRACTOR

TRAILER

TRUCK

PLATE VALIDATION

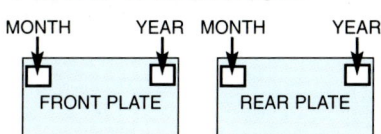

MONTH   YEAR   MONTH   YEAR

FRONT PLATE   REAR PLATE

YEAR EXPIRE **00**
VA 000000
00

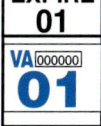

YEAR EXPIRE **01**
VA 000000
01

www.dmv.state.va.us

The "Old Dominion State" issues two fully-reflectorized license plates. Passenger plates are issued 3 alpha- 4 numeric, 3 alpha - 3 numeric, and all numeric plates. Virginia coined the term "communiplate" to promote personalized plate sales.Virginia has sold over 2 million special graphic optional plates which has generated over 20 million dollars of new revenue.

Distinctive captions:

DELEGATE - Member Virginia House of Delegates
DRIVE AWAY -Transporter / repossessor
HOBBYIST - Reconstructed car at least 20 years old
MILITARY ASSAULT FORCE- Member of any unit involved in combat (Desert Storm, Panama, Grenada etc.)

SHERIFF - Sheriff, private vehicle
POW - Former prisoner of war
POSTMASTER- Local postal official
REACT TEAM - Radio emergency group
RIDE SHARING - Car pool supporter of wildlife conservation

Codes:

Regular passenger car plates have 3 alpha -4 numeric and 3 alpha - 3 numeric characters. Trucks and other commercial vehicle plates have a 1 or 2 alpha prefix followed by numerics.

Alpha prefixes and suffixes reserved for special use:

AF	Air Force Reserve	**ID**	Import dealer	**RX**	Pharmacist
AR	Army Reserve	**L**	Local Govt. use	**TA-TZ**	Truck
CG	Coast Guard	**M**	Municipal	**TH**	Truck for hire
D	Dealer	**MC**	Motorcycle	**TR**	Trailer
DA	Drive-away	**MR**	Marine Reserve	**TRH**	Trailer for hire
E	Regular bus	**NG**	National Guard	**UD**	Used car dealer
EA	Apportioned bus	**NR**	Naval Reserve	**UR**	Univ. of Richmond
EQ	Equipment	**P**	Apportioned truck	**W&L**	Wash. & Lee Univ.
F	Farm truck	**PV**	Ride-sharing	**W&M**	Wm & Mary Univ.
FD	Franchised dealer	**PY**	Apportnd. tractor	**X**	Temporary tag
FM	Fran. mtr. home dlr.	**R**	Rental truck	**XA - XZ**	Tractor for hire
H	Taxi	**RT**	R.E.A.C.T. team	**Y**	Tractor
HA - HZ	Truck for hire	**RA**	Rental trailer	**YH**	Tractor for hire
HI	Hearing-impaired	**RAA-RZZ**	Rental passenger	**1A**	Lt. Governor
HO	Hobbyist	**RH**	Trailer for hire		
HP	Handicapped	**RS**	Rescue squad		

Passenger cars and trucks 7500 lbs and under are issued plates from these series:

1-10,000 (all numeric)

A2 - A10,000 (A1 issued to Attorney General)

AAA 1-ZZZ 999

T1 -T500 (pickup or panel truck only)

Commonwealth of Virginia, Department of Motor Vehicles
2300 West Broad Street, P.O.Box 27412, Richmond, VA 23269-0001
Tel. 804-367-0538

WASHINGTON

POLICE PATCH

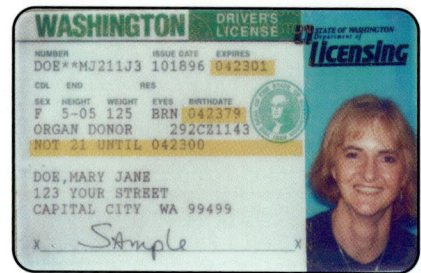

DRIVERS LICENSE

PASSENGER PLATES

PASSENGER 2
2 PLATES 2
DECALS

PASSENGER
OLDER BASE

PASSENGER
OLDER ISSUE

PERSONALIZED
OLDER ISSUE

HANDICAPPED

PERSONALIZED

TAX EXEMPT
CITY / STATE
VEHICLE

C.M.H

P.O.W.

PEARL
HARBOR
SURVIVOR

HULK HAULER

TRUCK AND TRAILER PLATES

TRUCK
APPORTONED

TRUCK

TRAILER

TRUCK
OLDER BASE

PLATE VALIDATION

MONTH   YEAR

FRONT PLATE   REAR PLATE

YEAR EXPIRE 00

YEAR EXPIRE 01

www.wsdot.wa.gov/

The "Evergreen State" issues two fully-reflectorized graphic license plates. Washington has not had a general plate re-issue since 1963 and there are five different bases currently in use. Personalized plates are available in a choice of three colors.

Distinctive captions:

DLR - Dealer
HORSELESS CARRIAGE - Vehicle manufactured in 1931 or earlier
HLK - Hulk hauler
MISC - Miscellaneous dealer
TRAN - Transporter
WKR - Wrecker / dismantler

XMT - Tax exempt - Government vehicle (including Indian tribal government) prefix or suffix: **D** -City-owned
C - County-owned
E, K, M - State-owned
I - Indian tribal-owned
WSP - Wash. State Patrol
SP- Wash. State Patrol

Codes:

Passenger vehicle plates have 3 alpha- 3 numeric and 3 numeric - 3 alpha characters. On older plates the first 2 alpha characters were a county code. Some of these plates are still in use but the codes are no longer accurate. The current issue of graphic plates have no county codes and on the most recent version the words *Centennial Celebration* no longer appear at the bottom.

The following numerics are assigned to these state officials:

1 Governor
2 Lt. Governor
3 Secretary of State

4 State Treasurer
5 State Auditor
6 Attorney General

7 Supt. Public Instruction
8 Land Commissioner
9 Insurance Commissioner

Truck, trailer, bus, publicly-owned and special vehicle plates have 1 or 2 alpha prefix (or suffix) which indicate as follows:

A	Truck	**HA - HZ**	Diesel truck	**T, U**	Truck	
B	State-owned	**J, JA - JZ**	Trailer	**TR**	Apportioned	
C	County	**L, LA - LZ**	Truck	trailer		
CC	Hon. Consul	**P, PA - PV**	Truck	**V**	Travel trailer	
DV	Disabled veteran	**Q ,Z**	Trailer	**W,WA-WZ**	Travel Trailer	
D OVER **P** Disabled person				**X, XA - XZ**	Truck	
F, FA-FZ	Trailer					
G, GA-GZ	Truck					

Washington State Department of Licensing, Bureau of Motor Vehicles
P.O.Box 48001, Olympia WA, 98504-8001   Tel. 360-902-3600

105

WEST VIRGINIA

POLICE PATCH

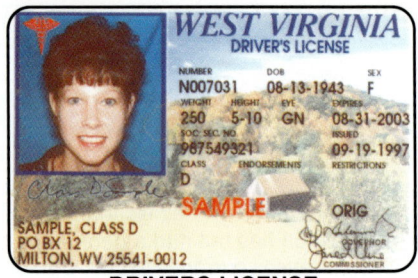

DRIVERS LICENSE

PASSENGER PLATES

PASSENGER
1 PLATE 1 DECAL

PERSONALIZED

DISABLED

**OPTIONAL
GRAPHIC**

EMS

**COLLEGIATE
UVW**

**COLLEGIATE
MARSHALL
UNIV.**

ENVIRONMENT

**NATIONAL
GUARD**

**COUNTY
OWNED**

**POLICE
ASSOCIATION**

SENATE

TRUCK AND TRAILER PLATES

**APPORTIONED
TRUCK**

**APPORTIONED
TRAILER -
LONG TERM**

**10 YEAR
TRAILER**

**APPORTIONED
TRAILER**

PLATE VALIDATION

MO/YR

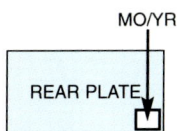

REAR PLATE

YEAR EXPIRE 00	YEAR EXPIRE 01

www.state.wv.us/wvdot

The "Mountain State" issues one fully-reflectorized graphic license plate. West Virginia issued a new base plate in 1996. A "scenic" plate is available for an additional fee.

Distinctive captions:

ANTIQUE CAR -Vehicle at least 25 years old

NON-RESIDENT - Non-residents with temporary and recurring business in the state of West Virginia

REPOSSESSOR - Vehicle repossessed by bank or lending institution

Codes:

All West Virginia class "A" plates (Passenger type motor vehicles and pickup trucks up to 8,000 lbs GVW other than those for hire) receive 1 numeric and 1 alpha, or 2 alpha prefix followed by 4 numerics.

The first character in the prefix indicates month of expiration. Plates expire on the *first* of :

1 - January	**4** - April	**7** - July	**O** - October
2 - February	**5** - May	**8** - August	**N** - November
3 - March	**6** - June	**9** - September	**D** - December

A second type of "A" plate is all numeric. Plate numbers 2 - 2,000 (without prefix) are assigned to individuals by the Governor. The Governor receives plate 1 and ONE.

Trucks, truck tractors and road tractors (other than those leased for hire) are issued plates with a B prefix followed by 1 - 5 numerics.
The numerics are for individual vehicle identification only. When registrations in this class exceed 5 figures, a small numeric indicating 100,000 is embossed under the B prefix.

All other vehicles are issued plates using a similar numbering system with an alpha prefix which indicates as follows:

C - Trailers, semi-trailers not for hire

D - Dealers (other alphas show type)

DV - Reserved for disabled veterans

E - Trucks , tractors exempt from
    Public Service Comm. jurisdiction

E over **S**- Emergency services

F over **F**- firefighter

H - Taxis and buses

J - Charter buses and cars

K - Leased or for hire trucks, tractors

L - Trailers, semi-trailers for hire

M over **U** - Marshall Univ. Alumni

O over **S**- Shriner

P over **S** - Penn State Alumni

R - House trailers

S - Special mobile equipment

T - Light trailers and semi-trailers
    (under1 Ton) drawn by pass. cars

POW - Ex prisoner of war

X - Farm truck

West Virginia does not designate the county of origin or weight of a vehicle on the license plate.

West Virginia Department of Transportation, Division of Motor Vehicles
Building 3, 1800 Kanawha Blvd., East, Charleston, WV 25317   Tel. 304-558-2723

WISONSIN

POLICE PATCH

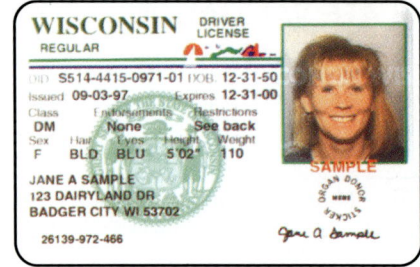

DRIVERS LICENSE

PASSENGER PLATES

PASSENGER
2 PLATES 2 DECAL
ON REAR

PERSONALIZED

DISABLED

HAM RADIO

ENVIRONMENT

SESQUICENTENNIAL

**COLLEGIATE
UNIV. OF WI.**
STANDARD DESIGN

**COLLEGIATE
UNIV. OF
WISCONSIN**

TRIBAL PLATE

**CHILDRENS
FUND**

STATE OWNED

**COUNTY
VEHICLE**

TRUCK AND TRAILER PLATES

APPORTIONED

**TRUCK
MULTI-YEAR**

SEMI-TRAILER

**TRUCK
PRIVATE
CARRIER**

PLATE VALIDATION

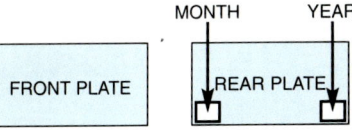

MONTH   YEAR

FRONT PLATE

REAR PLATE

YEAR EXPIRE **00**	YEAR EXPIRE **01**

www.dot.state.wi.us

"America's Dairyland" issues two fully-reflectorized license plates. A commemorative sesquicentennial graphic plate is available for an additional fee.

Distinctive captions:

ANTIQUE - 40-year- old vehicle
COLLECTOR - 20-year-old vehicle
DUAL PURPOSE VEH - Truck
also used as a motor home**.**
DUAL PURPOSE FARM - Truck
for farm and other uses

FINANCE CO - Repossessorl
HOBBYIST- Vehicle 20-years-old
reconstructed or homemade
OFFICIAL - State or municipal vehicle
used in law enforcement
TRANSF TRLR - Used to transport
modular-housing units

Codes:

Trucks and other commercial vehicle plates are clearly captioned to show class of vehicle such as truck, trailer. tractor, etc. However, on heavy vehicles the top alpha prefix is a code for the registered gross weight:

Z - 3,000 lbs	F - 20,000 lbs.	N - 56,000 lbs.
A - 4,500	G - 26,000	P - 62,000
B - 6,000	H - 22,000	Q - 68,000
C - 8,000	J - 38,000	R - 73,000
D - 12,000	K - 44,000	S - 76,000
E - 16,000	L - 50,000	T - 80,000

Wisconsin reserves the following prefix combinations for use on special plates:

BX - Bus (urban mass-transit system)
DIS - Disabled person
M over **H** - Mobile home
VET - Disabled veteran

X (suffix) - Vehicles registered at
    reduced fee.
ZY - Vehicle used to transport elderly
    and/or disabled persons.

BX - Bus (urban mass-transit system)
DIS - Disabled person
M over **H** - Mobile home
VET - Disabled veteran

X (suffix) - Vehicles registered at
    reduced fee.
ZY - Vehicle used to transport elderly
    and/or disabled persons.

Wisconsin Department of Transportation, Division of Motor Vehicles
4802 Sheboygan Avenue, P.O. Box 7911, Madison, WI 53707-7911   Tel. 608-266-2233

WYOMING

POLICE PATCH

DRIVERS LICENSE

PASSENGER PLATES

PASSENGER
NEW BASE
2000

PERSONALIZED

**DISABLED
VETERAN**

STATE OWNED

CITY OWNED

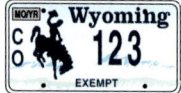

**COUNTY
OWNED**

**HIGHWAY
PATROL**

**AIR NATIONAL
GUARD**

FORMER POW

**PEARL
HARBOR
SURVIVOR**

**DEALER DEMO
PLATE**

**NATIONAL
GUARD**

TRUCK AND TRAILER PLATES

APPORTIONED

TRAILER

TRUCK

**APPORTIONED
TRAILER**

PLATE VALIDATION

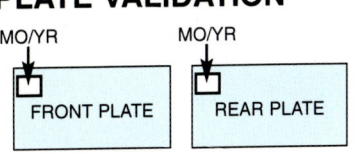

MO/YR — FRONT PLATE
MO/YR — REAR PLATE

WYOMING 3-00 00355869
WYOMING 3-01 00355869

www.state.wy.us

The "Equality State" issues two fully-reflectorized license plates. Wyoming has featured the bucking bronco on its plates continuously since 1936. A county code number appears to the left of the bronco.

Distinctive captions:

PIONEER - Vehicle at least 25 years old
COML - Commercial vehicle
SCHOOL - School district vehicle

Codes:

All Wyoming private and commercial license plates are issued by county treasurers and they have a numeric prefix which identifies the issuing county.

Wyoming has 23 counties and the prefix code, county and (county seat) are:

Prefix	County	County seat	Prefix	County	County seat
1	Natrona	Casper	13	Converse	Douglas
2	Laramie	Cheyenne	14	Niobrara	Lusk
3	Sheridan	Sheridan	15	Hot Springs	Thermopolis
4	Sweetwater	Rock Springs	16	Johnson	Buffalo
5	Albany	Laramie	17	Campbell	Gillette
6	Carbon	Rawlins	18	Crook	Sundance
7	Goshen	Torrington	19	Uinta	Evanston
8	Platte	Wheatland	20	Washakie	Worland
9	Big Horn	Basin	21	Weston	Newcastle
10	Fremont	Lander	22	Teton	Jackson
11	Park	Cody	23	Sublette	Pinedale
12	Lincoln	Kemmerer	99	Rental fleet vehicle	

Amateur radio, apportioned and pioneer plates have *no* county code.
Air National Guard plates have all *even* numerics; Army Guard has *odd* numerics.

State and other government owned vehicle plates have prefix codes. Multiple-character prefixes are stacked:

CC - Community college
CD - Civil Defense
CO - County-owned
EX - Vehicle exempt from fees
FD - Fire Dept.
GF - Game and Fish
GFD - Govt. Forestry Division

H - Highway Dept.
HD - Highway Dept. headquarters vehicle
HP - Highway Patrol
S - State-owned vehicle
UW - University of Wyoming-owned vehicles
WP - Weed and Pest Control

The following plates are manufactured without the bucking bronco symbol:
MFG - Manufacturer ,
TRL - Trailer, **DLR -** Dealer, **HT -** House trailer

Wyoming Department of Transportation, Licensing and Titling Section
P.O. Box 1708, Cheyenne, WY 82003-1708   Tel. 307-777-4709

ALBERTA

OPERATOR'S LICENCE

MOTORCYCLE

1 PLATE VALIDATED
BY 2 DECALS
CAN BE RE-VALIDATED
FOR 2 YR PERIOD

DRIVER'S LICENSE

PASSENGER REGULAR
3 ALPHA - 3 NUMERIC
(CLASS 3)

PERSONALIZED
2 PLATES ISSUED

DISABLED - WHEELCHAIR
DECAL IS OPTIONAL
PLATE BEGINS WITH "A"

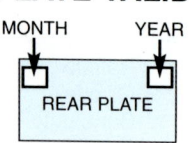

CLASS 1 PLATE
(PUBLIC SERVICE)

CLASS 2 PLATE, FARM
DECAL FOR PURPLE GAS

CLASS 4 PLATE

PLATE VALIDATION

MONTH   YEAR

REAR PLATE

YEAR EXPIRE 00

2000 SAMPLE

YEAR EXPIRE 01

2001 123456

www.gov.ab.ca/indexd

Alberta issues the same Wild Rose Country graphic design plate to all classes of vehicles. Whenever captions are used they appear on the upper right corner and are self-explanatory. Passenger car plates are 3 alpha - 3 numeric, and no codes are used.

Alberta has four regular classes and six special plates. The regular classes can be identified by a spacer dot •.

Class 1(Public Service vehicles) One numeric followed by a dot i.e. **1• 12345,** or 1 alpha and 5 numerics B-01234. Includes :Buses, livery, car rental, truck rental, public service trailer, driveaway

Class 2 2 numerics followed by dot , example. **46-A123.** Includes:Farm vehicle, nurseryman, Transport own goods,private. bus, Gen. merch. for hire.

Class 3 3 alpha dot 3 alpha i.e. **ABC•123.** Includes:Passenger, motorcycle, Govt, driveaway, transport own goods, commercial trailer.

Class 4 4 numerics dot 2 numerics i.e. **1234 • 56,** or 1 alpha, 3 numerics- 2 numerics: **A123-45** issued to :Trailers

Special plates are: Antique, Consular ,Dealer, Disabled, Ham radio. All are captioned

License plates are issued at random within a class, therefore it is not possible to distinguish between types. For example a rental car , a livery and a driveaway are all class 1 and have a single alpha or numeric prefix. Prefix VE6 is reserved for Ham radio operators. No other codes are used.

Alberta Registries
Motor Vehicle Division, Direct Customer Service
9th Floor, John E. Brownlee Bldg., 10365 97th St., Edmonton
Alberta, Canada T5J 3W7   Tel. 403-427-8250

BRITISH COLUMBIA

2 PLATES VALIDATED
BY 1 DECAL REAR PLATE

DRIVER'S LICENSE

MOTORCYCLE

PERSONALIZED

AMATEUR RADIO

FOREIGN CONSUL

COMMERCIAL TRUCK

APPORTIONED

ANTIQUE CAR

PLATE VALIDATION

MO/YR

FRONT PLATE

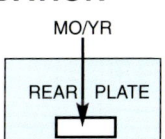

REAR PLATE

YEAR EXPIRE 00	YEAR EXPIRE 01

www.th.gov.bc.ca/
bchighways

* includes Yukon & N.W.T.

British Columbia issues 3 alpha - 3 numeric plates to passenger vehicles. There are no county of origin, weight or special use codes. The plate characters are for individual vehicle identification only.

Trucks, trailers and other commercial vehicle tags are 2 alpha - 4 numeric and these codes are used:

Prefix
A - Farm truck
D - Demonstrator
F - Farm tractor
MA- Auto-manufacturer
R - Repairer
P - Apportioned
TF - Trailer floater
TR - Transporter
X - Industrial equipment.
  The weight of a vehicle does not appear on a B.C.license plate.

Suffix
2 alpha - Commercial truck
1 Numeric 1 Alpha - Commercial trailer
SA - Special agreement plate- for mining
  equipment limited use of the highway.

Insurance Corporation of British Columbia (ICBC)
136 151 West Esplanade
North Vancouver, British Columbia V7M 3H9
Tel. 604-661-6348

MANITOBA

Passenger
2 plates

DRIVER'S LICENSE

MOTORCYCLE
DEALER

PASSENGER - 1983 ISSUE
2 PLATES

TAXI

PERSONALIZED CAN
BE ON 1983 OR 1987 BASE

PUBLIC SERVICE TRUCK

LOCAL TRUCK
SUFFIX BEGINS WITH
LETTER T,Y,Z

COMMERCIAL TRUCK

PLATE VALIDATION

DAY   MO/YR

↓REAR PLATE↓

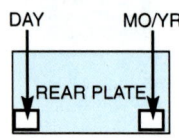

YEAR EXPIRE 00	YEAR EXPIRE 01

MB

www.gov.mb.ca

Manitoba issued a new graphic design plate to all vehicles during 1998. 2 plates per vehicle are required. Most plates are 3 alpha-3 numeric and special class identification stickers are used on some commercial plates. List of reserved plate prefixes and sticker symbols are below.

alpha prefix		Sticker codes	
C	Commercial		
CAL	Commercial trailer	CL	Country livrey
CC	Consular Corps	DA	Drive away
D	Dealer	LM	Limousine
P	Public service	F	Farm truck
PAL	Public service truck	T	Truck
R	Repairer	TX	Taxi, livrey
VE4	Amateur radio(Ham)	SV	Snow vehicle
X	Taxi, livery		

Manitoba Highways & Transportation
Division of Driver & Vehicle Licensing, 1075 Portage Ave.
Winnipeg, Manitoba R3G 0S1

NEW BRUNSWICK

2 PLATES VALIDATED
BY 1 DECAL ON BOTH PLATES

DRIVER'S LICENSE

MOTORCYCLE

conservation

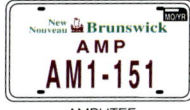

AMPUTEE

ANTIQUE AUTO

LIEUTENANT GOVERNOR

LT. COMMERCIAL VEHICLE

AMATEUR RADIO

TRAILER

LARGE COMMERCIAL VEHICLE

DIPLOMAT

PLATE VALIDATION

MO/YR   MO/YR

| FRONT PLATE | REAR PLATE |

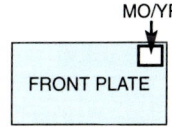
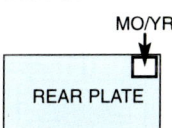

YEAR EXPIRE 00

YEAR EXPIRE 01

www.gov.nb.ca/dot/index.htm

New Brunswick issues 3 alpha - 3 numeric character plates to passenger cars, beginning at BAA-001. These plates were first issued May 1, 1991, and were used on all types of vehicles by april 1992. All types have uniform design.Light Commercial, truck ,tractor trailer and farm plates have a 1,2 or 3 alpha prefix code. .Special prefixes to look for on New Brunswick license plates:

AM - Amputee
D - Dealer
DP - Diplomat
CAA - CZZ - Lt. commercial vehicle
F - Farm truck
HA - Transporter
L - Large commercial vehicle
M - Miscellaneous

MC - Motorcycle
P - Farm produce transporter
PR - Pro rated vehicle
TA - Trailer
TAA - TZZ - Trailer
VE1 - Amateur Radio

New Brunswick Motor Vehicle Branch
P.O.Box 6000
Fredericton , N.B. E3B 5H1

115

NEWFOUNDLAND & LABRADOR

2 PLATES VALIDATED
BY 1 DECAL
ON REAR PLATE

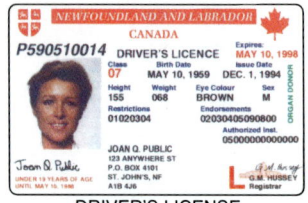

DRIVER'S LICENSE

MOTORCYCLE

PASSENGER REGULAR

500 YEAR COMMEMORATIVE

FEDERAL GOVT.
VEHICLE

EMERGENCY
VEHICLE

BUS

AMATEUR RADIO

PLATE VALIDATION

MO/YR   MO/YR

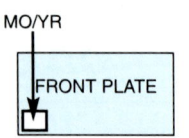

FRONT PLATE

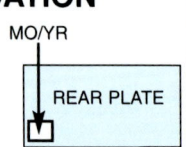

REAR PLATE

YEAR EXPIRE 00 — JULY

YEAR EXPIRE 01 — JULY

public.gov.nf.ca/wst

Newfoundland introduced the graphic plates(viking ship logo) in 1993, which will be phased in for all vehicles. Older plates. on issue since 1982, will continue to be used indefinitely. A limited edition "Cabot"commemorative plate is available for an additional fee.

Alpha prefixes with special meaning are:

CAA - CZZ - Commercial vehicle
BAA - BAZ - Bus
DAA - DAE - Dealer
EAA - EAZ - Emergency vehicle
FAA - FZZ - Farm, forestry,mining
GFA - GFZ - Federal government vehicle
GPA - GPZ - Provincial government

GMA - GMZ - Municipal government
MHA - Member of House Assembly
PRP - Prorated vehicle
TAA - TZZ - Trailer
TX - Taxi
W - Wrecker
XAA -XAZ - Construction equipment

Newfoundland & Labrador
Motor Registration Division, PO Box 8710
St. John's NF A1B 4J6   Tel. 709-729-2509

NOVA SCOTIA

2 PLATES VALIDATED
BY 2 DECALS
ON BOTH PLATES

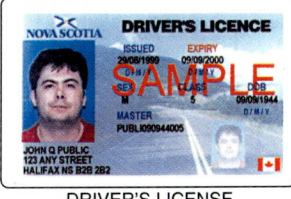

DRIVER'S LICENSE

MOTORCYCLE

PASSENGER
(OLD SERIES)

PASSENGER AND
LIGHT COMMERCIAL

PERSONALIZED

HANDICAPPED

PRORATE VEHICLE

HEAVY (OVER 5000 kg)
COMMERCIAL

TRAILER

FIREFIGHTER

NEW VEHICLE DEALER

PLATE VALIDATION

MO/YR   MO/YR   MO/YR   MO/YR

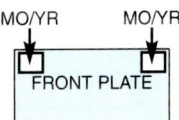
FRONT PLATE

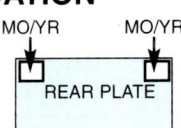
REAR PLATE

YEAR EXPIRE 00

YEAR EXPIRE 01

www.gov.ns.ca

All Nova Scotia plates are used for many years and revalidated by decals. Passenger plates have 3 alpha - 3 numeric characters and have no codes. The most recent issue is (Schooner "Bluenose"), however older passenger plates are still on the road. Heavy trucks, trailers and other commercial vehicles over 5000 Kg. have black on yellow. Government vehicle plates are black on beige, and prorated plates red on yellow. The alpha prefixes reserved for special use:

D -New car dealer)
F over M - Farm /fisherman truck)
F over T - farm tractor
F over F(suffix)-Firefighter
G over T - General tractor

PR -Prorated
P over T - Semi-trailer
R - Government
T - Trailer
U - Used car dealer
VE1-Amateur radio

Nova Scotia Department of Transportation
Registry of Motor Vehicles, 6061 Young St
Halifax, NS B3J 2Z3

ONTARIO

DRIVER'S LICENSE

MOTORCYCLE

2 PLATES VALIDATED BY 1 DECAL
ON REAR PLATE OF PASSENGER
AND FRONT PLATE OF
COMMERCIAL VEHICLES

PASSENGER REGULAR
3 ALPHA - 3 NUMERIC

FEDERAL GOVERNMENT

PERSONALIZED

DIPLOMATIC CORPS.

ONTARIO GOVERNMENT

MEMBERS OF HOUSE
OF COMMONS

SENATOR

DEALER

AMATEUR RADIO

PLATE VALIDATION

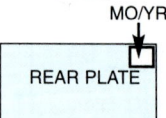

MO/YR

FRONT PLATE	REAR PLATE

YEAR EXPIRE 00	YEAR EXPIRE 01

www.mto.gov.on.ca/
english

Most Ontario license plates have 6 or 7 characters divided by a crown.
Passenger are 3 or 4 numeric - 3 alpha . Earlier issue 3 alpha 3 numeric plates
are still in use. Passenger plates are blue on white, commercial are black on white
and diplomatic white on red.Many special sport and collegiate plates are available.The
following alpha prefix and (suffix) combinations have special meaning:

*CAN (prefix or suffix) -Fed. govt cabinet
 (CCA) - Consular Corps (white on red)
 (CDA) - Diplomatic Corps (white on red)
 (DCO) - District Court Judge (sfx)
*FCJ - Fed. Court Judge
*FDA - Federal Govt vehicle
*HVA - Historic vehicle
*MDA,MDZ - Medical doctor
*MHC - Member House Commons
*MPP - Ontario legislature

ONZ - Ontario govt. veh
*ONT - Ontario govt cabinet
*PJO - Ontario provincial Judge
*SCO - Ont. Supreme Court Judge
*SEN - Senate members Fed Govt.
*TRB - Tax Review Board
VE3 (prefix only) - Amateur Radio

*can be either prefix or suffix

Ontario Ministry of Transportation
Safety and Regulation Division, 1201 Wilson Ave. East Bldg.
Downsview ON, M3M 1J8   Tel. 1-800-auto-PL8

PRINCE EDWARD ISLAND

ONE PLATE, 2 DECALS
CONFEDERATION BRIDGE

DRIVER'S LICENSE

MOTORCYCLE

Province House plate

Amateur radio

PERSONALIZED

MEMBER OF LEGISLATURE

FIREFIGHTER

HEAVY TRUCK (4500kg)

PUBLIC VEHICLE

PRORATED VEHICLE

former graphic

PLATE VALIDATION

MO/YR

REAR PLATE

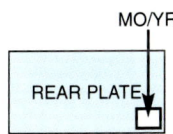

YEAR EXPIRE 00

02/00
004138

YEAR EXPIRE 01

01/01
004138

www2.gov.pe.ca/tpw/index

These alpha prefixes are reserved for special use:

Commercial Truck
DLR - Dealers
F- Farm vehicle
FD- Firefighter
G - Government service
M - Motorcycle
PV - Public vehicle
SBA to **SBB**- School bus
SV - Service vehicle
SNOWMOBILE
OFF HIGHWAY

T- Trailer
TV-1/3 year heavy truck
VY2 - Ham radio call letters
XM- Citizens band radio

Prince Edward Island
Department of Transportation
PO Box 2000, Charlottetown, PEI C1A 7NS
Tel. 902-368-5200

QUEBEC

1 PLATE , QUEBEC NO LONGER
VALIDATES PLATES
WITH DECALS ON PLATES

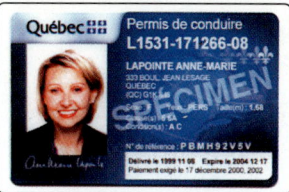

DRIVER'S LICENSE

MOTORCYCLE

HANDICAPPED PERSON
WHEELCHAIR STICKER
UPPER RT. HAND CORNER

COMMERCIAL VEHICLE

RESTRICTED TRAVEL PLATE
(COLLECTOR VEHICLE)

TRUCK

TRUCK PERMANENT PLATE

TRUCK PRORATED

DEALER

BUS

CONSULAR OFFICIAL

PLATE VALIDATION

YEAR EXPIRE 00	YEAR EXPIRE 01
NO VALIDATION DECALS USED	NO VALIDATION DECALS USED

NO VALIDATION DECALS USED

www.gouv.qc.ca

Quebec license plates all use the same design.Passenger plates are
3 alpha- 3 numeric and have no hidden codes. Other categories of plates have
an alpha prefix which identifies the class and numerics that identifies the
particular vehicle. All Quebec license plates are permanent.

A - Buses: Public, private, school
C - Vehicles with restricted right of travel.
CC - Consular corps
CD - Diplomatic Corps
F - Commercial vehicles
R - Trailers
T - Urban taxi

TR - Rural taxi
TS - Limousine
L - General merchandise transport
V - All terrain
VE2 - Ham radio
VR - Bulk transport
X - Floater license plate.

Societe de l'assurance automobile du Quebec
333 Boulevard Jean-Lesage, C.P.19600
Quebec, PQ G1K 8J6
Tel. 418-528-3230

SASKATCHEWAN

2 PLATES VALIDATED BY CLASS
OF VEHICLE DECAL ON LOWER LEFT
AND YEAR DECAL LOWER RIGHT

DRIVER'S LICENSE

MOTORCYCLE

LT. GOVERNOR

MEDICAL DOCTOR

PERSONALIZED

DISABLED

COMMERCIAL TRUCK

FARM TRUCK

GOVERNMENT

COMMERCIAL TRAILER

LEASED VEHICLE

PLATE VALIDATION

DAY   MO/YR

REAR PLATE

REAR PLATE

YEAR EXPIRE 00	YEAR EXPIRE 01
SASK JAN	N/A

www.engr.usask.ca/tc/
skhwy

Saskatchewan license plates have 6 characters, 3 alpha- 3 numeric with a graphic wheat design separating the two groupings. The only exception is personalized and disabled person plates which have different character configurations and the wheat does not appear.. Different color alpha coded stickers are used to indicate the class of vehicle:

Green on White stickers
PV - Private vehicle
T - Private trailer
GC - Government veh.
Blue on White Stickers
A - Commercial
AG - Public serv.veh
     restricted use.

C - Commercial /
    restricted
D - Commercial/
    provincial
TS - Commercial
    trailer
L - Leased
LT - Leased trailer

PB - Public bus
PC - City bus
PS - School bus
PT - Public taxi
TS - Commercial
    trailer
Red on White
F - Farm

Saskatchewan Auto Fund
Government Insurance
2260 11th Ave., Regina, SK S4P 2N7
Tel. 306-787-4032

NORTHWEST TERRITORIES & NUNAVUT

10635
NORTHWEST TERRITORIES
2 PLATES VALIDATED
BY 2 DECALS

DRIVER'S LICENSE

LZ 999
MOTORCYCLE

123N
NUNAVUT
Nunavut 2 plates

C 1234
NORTHWEST TERRITORIES
COMMERCIAL

P 1234
NORTHWEST TERRITORIES
PUBLIC SERVICE
(TRUCK)

G123
NORTHWEST TERRITORIES
GOVERNMENT
OWNED VEHICLE

D123
NORTHWEST TERRITORIES
DEALER

R123
NORTHWEST TERRITORIES
RENTAL VEHICLE

T1234
NORTHWEST TERRITORIES
TRAILER

VE8AA
NORTHWEST TERRITORIES
AMATEUR RADIO

S 1234
NORTHWEST TERRITORIES
SCHOOL BUS

PLATE VALIDATION

DAY   MO/YR

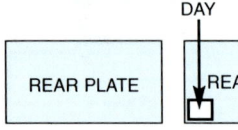
REAR PLATE

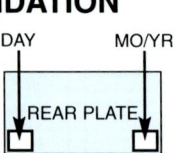
REAR PLATE

YEAR EXPIRE 00
00
1234567

YEAR EXPIRE 01
01
1234567

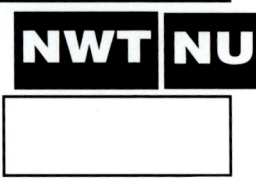
NWT NU

All Northwest Territories and Nunavut plates are in the shape of a polar bear. Regular passenger vehicle plates are all numeric and the numbers have no other significance other than to identify the individual vehicle. Nunavut plates have an N suffix. Commercial, government and other vehicle plates have a 1 alpha prefix code:

N.W.T does not issue special plates to disabled persons.

C - Commercial Vehicle
D - Dealer
E - Public service vehicle (exempt)
G - Government owned vehicle

P - Public service vehicle (truck)
R - Rental vehicle (Hertz etc.)
S - School bus
T -Trailer   **VE8** - Ham radio

NORTHWEST TERRITORY DEPT. OF TRANSPORTATION
MOTOR VEHICLE DIVISION
PO BOX 1320, YELLOWKNIFE, NWT XJA 2L9
Tel. 403-667-8633

NUNAVUT
DIV. OF MOTOR VEHICLES
PO BOX 207
GJOA HAVEN, Nunavut
XOE150
867-360-6339

YUKON TERRITORY

1 PLATE VALIDATED BY
2 DECALS

DRIVER'S LICENSE

MOTORCYCLE

PERSONALIZED
2 PLATES ISSUED

PASSENGER OLDER ISSUE
miner has been used since 1952

ROYAL CDN
MTD POLICE

YUKON TERRITORIAL
GOVERNMENT

FEDERAL GOVERNMENT

RENTAL VEHICLE

LIGHT COMMERCIAL VEHICLE

HEAVY COMMERCIAL VEHICLE

DEALER

PLATE VALIDATION

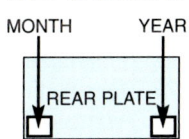

MONTH   YEAR

REAR PLATE

YEAR EXPIRE 00

00
234567

YEAR EXPIRE 01

01
234567

www.gov.yk.ca/depts.html

Yukon Territory passenger plates have 3 alpha - 1 or 2 numeric characters. They have no codes. However the renewal month is assigned by the first initial of the owner's last name or the first letter of a corporate name.Other classes of vehicles can be identified by the alpha prefix on the plate:

C - Commercial
D,DLR - Dealer
F - Farm
G, YTG - Yukon Government
M - Motorcycle, moped
R - Rented vehicle
S - Snowmobile
T - Trailer
VE9- Ham radio call letters

First letter of name / word	Renew Mo.
F or H	January
M	February
B	March
D,V,O or E	April
N or T	May
W, Y, or R	July
K,J, or I	August
C, Q, or X	September
A or P	October
S,U, or Z	November
G or L	December

Yukon Territory
Community & Transportation Services
PO Box 2703, 308 Steele St.
White Horse, YT Y1A 2C6   Tel. 403-667-570203

MEXICO

States of Mexico

1. Aguascalientes (AGS)
2. Baja California (BC)
3. Baja California Sur (BCS)
4. Campeche (CAMP)
5. Chiapas (CHIS)
6. Chihuahua (CHIH)
7. Coahuila (COAH)
8. Colima (COL)
9. Durango (DGO)
10. Federal District (Mexico City) (DF)
11. Guanajuato (GTO)
12. Guerrero (GRO)
13. Hildago (HGO)
14. Jalisco (JAL)
15. Mexico (MEX)
16. Michoachan (MICH)
17. Morelos (MOR)
18. Nayarit (NAY)
19. Nuevo Leon (NL)
20. Oaxaca (OAX)
21. Puebla (PUE)
22. Queretaro (QRO)
23. Quintana Roo (QR)
24. San Luis Potosi (SLP)
25. Sinaloa (SIN)
26. Sonora (SON)
27. Tabasco (TAB)
28. Tamaulipas (TAMPS)
29. Tlaxcala (TLAX)
30. Veracruz (VER)
31. Yucatan (YUC)
32. Zacatecas (ZAC)

Mexico issues 2 license plates to passenger vehicles. The authorities provide a small decal of the exact plate which is attached to the windshield as security measure. The states that border USA (BC, SON, CHIH. COAH. and TAMPS) have a distinctive yellow FRONTERA license plate for vehicles that operate within 20 miles of the border. All private passenger cars have traditionally had the same design- 3 or 4 letters and numbers most recently green on white. The letters and numbers are issued by series within the state. But starting in 1998 distinctive graphics plates began to appear... These colorful new plate designs seen on the highways is positive evidence of the variety of culture and change in the states of modern Mexico. The spotting of the different license plates of Mexico is a favorite activity for travelers of all ages. We include a selection of these new and old plate designs for your "collecting" enjoyment.

MEXICO (PRIVATE AUTO PLATES SHOWN EXCEPT WHERE INDICATED)

Aguascalientes

Baja California

Baja California
FRONTERA

Baja California Sur
Trailer

Campeche

Campeche
Taxi

Chiapas

Coahuila

Coahuila
FRONTERA

Chihuahua

Chihuahua
FRONTERA

Colima

Distrito Federal

Durango
Truck

Guanajuato

MEXICO

Guerrero

Hidalgo

Jalisco

Mexico

Michoacan

Morelos

Nayrit
Truck

Nuevo Leon

Oaxaca

Puebla
Trailer

Queretaro

Quintana Roo

San Luis Potosi

Sinaloa

Sonora

MEXICO

Tabasco

Tamaulipas

Tamaulipas
FRONTERA

Tamaulipas
FRONTERA TAXI

Tlaxcala

Veracruz

Veracruz
Truck

Yucatan

Zacatecas

**Auto Collector
Distrito Federal**

**Auto Collector
Puebla**

Publications for ID Pubco

CD ROM 1999

PlateTracer CD an electronic license plate quick check of auto, truck and semi-trailer plates in color on cd rom. Trace any plate back to the issuing jurisdiction when only the type of vehicle and plate colors are known. They can be sorted by state, color and vehicle type. A critical tool for motor vehicle investigation particularly when working with witnesses. Price *($50) PlateTracer CD* contact IDPUBCO.

NEW CD ROM 2000

PlateTracer CD Broadcast Edition a complete "Colorbank" of all U.S. and Canada license plates in use during yr. 2000. Designed for television and general media use, over 800 current license plate images can be reviewed one at a time or sorted by state and/or category such as regular passenger, handicapped, military, commercial and special causes including environment and wildlife. Appropriate selected plates may be exported to the clipboard and customized for broadcast or use in print. Contact IDPUBCO for full details and availability.

OTHER PUBLICATIONS

The Official License Plate Book	$16.95 ea.
The License Plate Game	$5.00 ea.
The Road Sign Game	$5.00 ea.
World Cards	$12.95 per set
License Plate Quick-Check 2000	$2.00 ea.

To order contact Interstate Directory Publishing, 420 Jericho Turnpike, Jericho, NY 11753 ph: 1-800-347-0473, fax: 516-822-5966 website: www.idpubco.com, email: info@idpubco.com. Mastercard & Visa.

DO YOU COLLECT LICENSE PLATES?
The Automobile License Plate Collectors Association (ALPCA)
can be reached through the secretary treasurer
Mr. Gary Brent KINCADE
P.O. Box 7
Horner, WV 26372